LANTERNS AND LIFEBOATS

To Joe & Pam –

Islands are for Adventure!

Steve Tongue

LANTERNS AND LIFEBOATS

A HISTORY OF THUNDER BAY ISLAND

STEPHEN D. TONGUE

Illustrations by Diane L. Tongue

This project was made possible with support from:

Michigan Council for the Arts and Cultural Affairs
Cheboygan Area Arts Council Regranting Agency
Community Foundation of Northeast Michigan
Wal-Mart
Michigan Humanities Council,
an affiliate of the National
Endowment for the Humanities

Photography by Thane
Riverside Framing & Gallery

Cover photos courtesy of Thunder Bay Island Preservation Society - Life Saving Station in 1886

Cover design by Thane Whitscell

Sarge Publications
829 W. Chisholm Street
Alpena, MI 49707

Library of Congress Control Number: 2004094189
ISBN 0-9758902-0-4

Sweet, dear little Isle of the sea!
The grand old waves shall dash upon thy shore
When we who once have trod thy lovely beach
Shall be known to earth no more

-Elizabeth Williams, *A Child of the Sea*

CONTENTS

PREFACE

"The islands were basically the 19th century equivalent of today's freeway exits. Instead of gas stations, the steam powered ships ...refueled with wood...and island entrepreneurs offered food, lodging and a place to hide from the storms."

-Gary Volgenau, Detroit Free Press, July 7, 2002.

An island's remoteness enhances its intrigue. While only four miles from land, Thunder Bay Island seems a world away. The earliest settlers of Thunder Bay called this island their home, yet it is not even visible from Alpena and has, in a sense, been forgotten by all except a faithful few who are endeavoring to preserve it. Such seclusion was remarked by many early visitors. Fred Landon's book, Lake Huron, relates two accounts. There are the journals of a "Victorian Lady," Anna Jameson, travelling up Lake Huron during the summer of 1847 on the steamboat *Thomas Jefferson.* She described the Thunder Bay Island lighthouse as "*terrific in its solitude.*" Similarly, there is the narrative of Frederick Starin of New York travelling to Wisconsin on the *Constellation* in 1840:

About 7 o'clock the boat stopped off Thunder Bay Island, but no signal being discovered on shore she again proceeded on her journey. There is a lighthouse and comfortable dwelling on the southern extremity of this island where there are a few acres cleared. The rest of it is one dense forest, and really a bleak, lonely, desolate place. About the middle I discovered a few miserable huts, probably the abodes of fishermen, saw several other small islands between it and the main land, all thickly wooded.

Though remote, in time and place, Thunder Bay Island's stories should not be forgotten. I have chosen to present this history by topic, rather than chronologically. Each chapter deals with a different subject including the fishermen, lighthouse, lifesaving station, shipwrecks, and recent preservation efforts. I have also expanded the history to place the island in the context of our rich Great Lakes maritime legacy.

——————— - ———————

There are many whose contributions made this project possible. I want to acknowledge the following for their assistance and resources:

Alpena County Library
Clarke Historical Library – Central Michigan University
Jesse Besser Museum
Michigan Maritime Museum
Thunder Bay Island Preservation Society
Thunder Bay National Marine Sanctuary

Appreciation goes to those I interviewed who shared information and memories of the island. I would also like to thank Sue Skibbe and Herb Palmer of the Thunder Bay Island Preservation Society for their encouragement as well as Shawn Sexton, Phil Cook and Fred Stonehouse for editorial assistance. Deep gratitude goes to my wife, Amy, for her support. Finally, I dedicate this book to my father, David Tongue, who nurtured both a thirst for adventure and an appreciation of God's marvelous creation – the Great Lakes.

CHAPTER I – NATURAL HISTORY

In 1854, government surveyor Thomas Whelphy surveyed Thunder Bay Island. His description sets the stage for a look at the island's natural history:

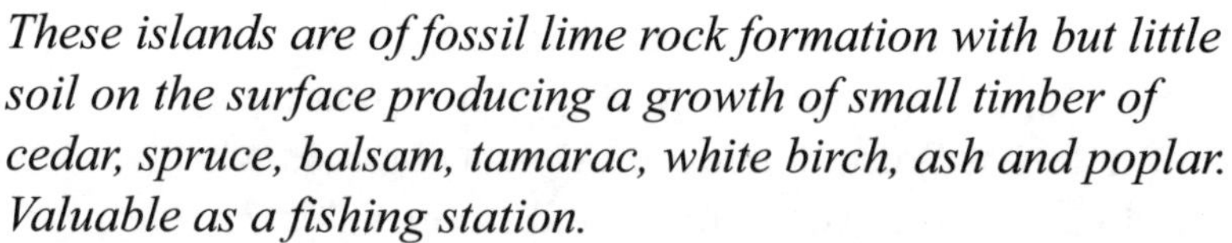

These islands are of fossil lime rock formation with but little soil on the surface producing a growth of small timber of cedar, spruce, balsam, tamarac, white birch, ash and poplar. Valuable as a fishing station.

According to paleontologists, the limestone forming the bedrock in the Thunder Bay region was created during the Middle Devonian era. This rock is part of a formation called the Traverse Group, and it protrudes along the shoreline of Lakes Huron and Michigan at roughly the same latitude. The limestone and shale originated from shallow seas where a high concentration of sea animals created a calcium carbonate precipitate. This has graced Thunder Bay with a rich abundance of fossils and the high quality limestone and shale that would figure prominently in Alpena's economic future.

The first State Geologist of Michigan, Douglass Houghton, did not recognize the value of this limestone during his early surveys. From reports he made between 1837-1845 he described the island as follows:

Outer Thunder Bay island is composed of limestone, covered in part, by a very thin deposit, chiefly of vegetable matter. An inferior coarse of building stone may be obtained, in considerable quantities, upon this island, but it is extremely irregular in shape and not of the most durable character. The southerly portion of outer Thunder Bay island is composed of a shelly or sub-slaty, silicious limestone, considerably charged with bitumen and almost wholly composed of a congeries of fossils....it possesses much interest in a scientific point of view, but is of no value for any practical purposes.

Paleontologists have assigned names to the various layers of rock in the Traverse Formation. The rock surfacing at Thunder Bay Island is classified as the "Killians member" of the 116-foot thick Genshaw strata. The Killians outcrop forms a ridge running from northwest to southeast across Montmorency, Presque Isle and Alpena counties which, according to geologists Warthin and Cooper, *"forms the edge of the platform on which Gull, Sugar and Thunder Bay islands rest."* This is a geological fault line, which winds its way across northeastern Michigan, leaving a path of unusual formations such as sinkholes and cuestas. This same fault has created a dramatic underwater cliff along the eastern side of the island.

The Genshaw limestone forms the foundation of Thunder Bay Island, but it was glaciers that carved out the Great Lakes and landscape of Thunder Bay. From about 11,000 to 4,000 years ago, lake levels fluctuated greatly, and the island would have been submerged some times and linked to the mainland at others. Geologists believe that Thunder Bay assumed its present shape approximately 2,500 years ago.

The exposed bedrock of Thunder Bay Island has drawn international attention for its rare "alvar" ecosystem. An alvar occurs on flat bedrock "pavements" which have shallow soils. They are subjected to extremes of both flooding and drought and create a habitat for rare species of plant and animal life. Alvars occur at only three locations in the world:

the Baltic region, County Clare in Ireland, and the Great Lakes. Researchers have been cataloguing these ecosystems for preservation. The most recent study (1994 – 1997) was sponsored by the International Alvar Conservation Institute and the Michigan Natural Features Inventory. The final report identified the following rare species:

Butterwort (Pinguicula vulgaris)
Calypso Orchid (Calypso bulbosa)
Ram's Head Ladyslipper (Cypripedium ariertinum)
Dwarf Lake Iris (Iris lacustris)
Douglas' Hawthorn (Crataegus douglasii)
Sedge (Carex scirpoidea)
False Pennyroyal (Trichostema brachiatum)

Also noted were nesting sites for the following birds:

Caspian Tern (Sterna caspia)
Common Tern (Sterna hirundo)
Ring Billed Gulls (Larus delawarensis)

These natural features of Thunder Bay Island led to its inclusion in the Michigan Islands National Wildlife Refuge, a unit within the Shiawassee National Wildlife Refuge.

They have also led to its 1996 designation in the Misery Bay Biodiversity Investment Area. The State of the Lakes Ecosystem Conference, a joint venture of Environment Canada and the U.S. Environmental Protection Agency (EPA), thus recognized the shorelines in this area as having "*exceptionally high ecological values which warrant exceptional attention to protect from degradation.*" Consequently, in 2003, the EPA funded the "Misery Bay Initiative" which has begun the process of developing a long-range plan for protection of the unique habitats of these shorelines.

As we now turn to the human story of Thunder Bay Island, we will see how it is intertwined with the natural history and features, notably:

*A fishing heritage tied to the surrounding reefs and fertile fishing grounds

*Proximity to navigational lanes and treacherous underwater hazards which required a lighthouse and life saving station.

CHAPTER II – EARLY HISTORY

It is believed that the first human contact with Thunder Bay Island would have been Great Lakes Native Americans between the Late Archaic and Late Woodland periods. While most Native American activities in the Thunder Bay region took place along the Thunder Bay River, the islands would have been important for fishing.

By the early 1800's, the upper Great Lakes were populated by three Native American groups: the Ottawa in the West, the Potawatomi in the South and the Ojibwa (or Chippewa) in the East. As hunters and fishermen, the Chippewa were at home in Thunder Bay with its abundance of wildlife and fish. In his 1820 Journal, Henry Schoolcraft mentions a native campsite at North Point (Shoshekonawbegonking) which likely served as a base for fishing the nearby waters surrounding the islands.

The first Europeans to explore the Great Lakes were the French, but it is doubtful that any of the early explorers such as Brule, Champlain, or Nicolet sighted Thunder Bay Island. Their routes traversed the Georgian Bay region to the upper Lakes. They purposely avoided the lower portions of the Great Lakes due to the hostility of the Iroquois who populated this region.

The best guess is that Adrien Joliet was the first European to see Thunder Bay during his paddle along the eastern side of Lake Huron in 1669. Later, in 1679, French priest Louis Hennepin described Thunder Bay Island in his journal. He was accompanying LaSalle's 45-ton ship *Griffin* en route to

Green Bay from Niagara to collect furs. According to Hennepin, they had just weathered a squall while journeying north out of Saginaw Bay and finally found relief when "*becalmed in two fathoms among Thunder Bay Islands*."

From the 1660's to 1796, the Great Lakes were caught in a political and economic struggle for power between the French and British. The French were largely in control from 1669 – 1760, but the British ultimately asserted authority over the region at the conclusion of the French and Indian War. During this period, Thunder Bay played a minor role as an outpost for fur traders. They typically arrived in the fall, spending their winter trading with the natives by the rivers. In spring they loaded their supply of furs on the "Montreal Barges" that were paddled along the Great Lakes shoreline.

Throughout this period, the settlements and forts established at Mackinac became the locus of influence and power in the region. While the Revolutionary War ended in 1783, it was not until the 1796 Jay Treaty when British forces withdrew from the region. By this time, Michigan was part of the Northwest Territory. In 1805, Congress created the Michigan Territory and the last flourish of fur trading took place under the authority of the American Fur Company organized by Astor and managed from Mackinac Island. In 1828, Ephraim and Gordon Williams were appointed to operate the post at Saginaw. From here, they traveled up Lake Huron as far as Thunder Bay on their sloop, *Savage,* to collect furs. However, by the early 1830's, the fur trading business was shifting westward and largely on the decline in the Great Lakes. A new era began as the Great Lakes became the conduit for our nation's expansion. And as ships carried the settlers westward, the Thunder Bay Island lighthouse would guide them along their way.

CHAPTER III – LIGHTHOUSE

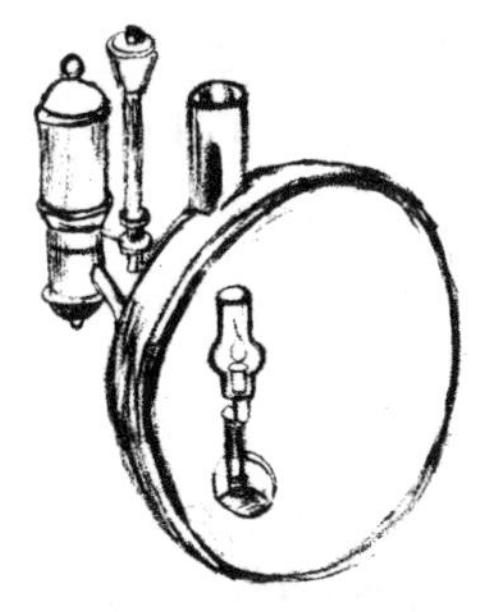

"The most barren, inhospitable residence I have ever yet had...I think it will be many years before this part of the U.S. is settled."

-Diary of stonemason Henry West – during construction of the Thunder Bay Island lighthouse in 1831.

David D. Oliver, in his book Centennial History of Alpena County, gives an account and description of the first settlers to Thunder Bay Island. Oliver was part of an 1839 surveying crew hired by Lewis Clason and Thomas Patterson, and contracted by the State of Michigan to survey townships in the northern part of the state. In 1815, government surveyors had established the base line and prime meridian from which subsequent surveys would be based. By 1825, the southern third of the Lower Peninsula had been surveyed, but it would take over twenty-five more years to survey the rest of the state.

Map of Thunder Bay, Sugar and Gull Islands

The surveying crews departed from Pontiac in April 1839. They traveled by wagon, foot, boat and scow to the northern wilderness. Clason and Patterson split the group in two: Clason's party landed at the Au Sable River and Patterson's at the Devil River. The standard surveying party of the day consisted of four men: the surveyor, two chainmen and an axeman. They spent the season laying out township lines through a wilderness of swamp, streams, lakes, hills and woods. It was fairly lucrative work for its day, with a crew earning $3000 at the end of the season to split amongst themselves. At the conclusion of their season's surveying tasks, Clason brought his party up to the Devil River where they assembled with the Patterson party to "*determine how to get home*." The solution: take advantage of Thunder Bay Island's proximity to Lake Huron boat traffic and find a schooner bound for Detroit.

With Pete Wawatum, a Native American guide, Oliver and the others paddled the fifteen miles across Thunder Bay in a birch-bark canoe to Thunder Bay Island. When they arrived at the island, they were treated to the hospitality of Jesse Muncey, lighthouse keeper and fisherman. He was described as a "*very clever and kindly*" man. This group of surveyors, and the lighthouse keeper's family, enjoyed breaking the isolation of their respective occupations by sharing whitefish that Muncey had gill netted off the island.

Muncey's lighthouse at Thunder Bay Island was only the third to be built on Lake Huron. In 1789, the very first "public works" project authorized by Congress created the Lighthouse Establishment. From 1813 to 1820, the first lighthouses were constructed on the Great Lakes. The Thunder Bay Island lighthouse had the misfortune of being constructed in 1831 - a time when lighthouse appropriations had been delegated to the "Fifth Auditor of the Treasury."

This was a low point in lighthouse history since the auditor strangled funding, and many of the structures constructed at this time were substandard.

According to Alpena historian Fred Trelfa, the 1830 Congress appropriated $5000 to establish a lighthouse on "Outer Thunder Bay Island." In March 1831, Stephen Pleasonton, 5th Auditor, requested that Adam D. Stewart, Collector of Customs at Michilimackinac, select the site:

Treasury Department
Fifth Auditors Office
15 March, 1831

Sir,
At the last session of congress, the following appropriations were made for objects in relation to the Light House establishment within the range of your superintendence, viz:

1. For a Light House at the mouth of Chicago River, Lake Michigan...$5000

2. For a Light House at the confluence of the St. Joseph's River with Lake Michigan...$5000

3. For a Light House on the Outerthunder Bay Island in Lake Huron...$5000

4. For a Light Boat to be stationed in the Strait connecting Lakes Huron and Michigan...$10,000

5. For Buoys and placing the same on the flats at the head of Lake St. Clair...$350

I have to request that you will lose no time in selecting the most suitable sites for the Light Houses. It is understood that the land at Chicago River and Outerthunder Bay Island already belongs to the Government. If you find this to be the fact, measures may be immediately taken for erecting the buildings. For this purpose I enclose advertisements of proposals for a Light House of sixty five feet at each place... I have the honor to be very respectfully, Your most obedient servant,

S. Pleasonton
Fifth Auditor
Acting Commissioner of the Revenue

The location of Thunder Bay made good sense for a number of reasons. First, there were the limestone reefs that created underwater hazards. Secondly, Thunder Bay Island was a natural turning point between the largely north/south route on the lower lake and the west/east route on the upper lake. Furthermore, boat traffic tended to be more concentrated at this "pinch point" in the shipping lanes. In addition, Thunder Bay had always been a natural refuge for boat traffic from the northwest gales that could blow immense seas. Finally, by positioning the lighthouse on the island, the radius of visibility was easily 220 degrees and would be seen from as far north as Middle Island and as far south as South Point.

Advertisements for bids to construct a lighthouse ran that spring with the bids to be forwarded to the Treasury Department. In May, Stewart was advised that the bid of Henry T. Blake[1] was lowest and a contract was authorized for building a lighthouse and dwelling house for $3244 and fit out for $650. A crew of twelve arrived in July and went to work. Henry West, a stonemason on the project wrote in his diary of daily life on the island including "*the never ending roar of Lake Huron breaking on the rocks.*" He described the trading that went on with the local Indians (they traded pork and flour for pigeons that the Indians caught). "*The greatest deprivation is I cannot hear from my old acquaintances as I neither get letters or paper.*" He was hired at $1.75 per day

[1] Later documents list Jeremiah Moors as the builder.

"plus a quantity of sugar."

However, all did not proceed smoothly. Beginning in September, a series of storms swept over the island. On November 30, 1831, Eber Ward, lighthouse keeper at Bois Blanc Island, wrote to his daughter Emily:

I forgot to tell you that as the workers were doing the last work to the Thunder Bay Light it fell to the ground. The workmen discovered it was on the point of falling just in time to escape a terrific death. It fell in consequence of the waves dashing against it and washing out all the mortar to the height of ten or fifteen feet.

Similarly on December 29, 1831, the Erie *Gazette* reported:

We regret to learn that the Light Houses which were to have been completed this fall at Chicago and Thunderbay Island have both fallen down.

In 1832, Henry West gave his own eyewitness account:

The tower fell before quite completed and with it all our hope... as yet I have never received a single cent nor do I think I ever shall...it was owing to the storms and tempests and the exposed situation of the tower that it fell...the spray washing over it was thirty feet high.

This delayed completion until October 1832, when $4450 was requested to pay the contractor for his services. But the destruction of the first tower led to a petition by the contractor "*praying compensation for loss sustained in building a lighthouse on Outer thunder bay island, which fell in consequence of being located on a site unfit for the same."*

Jesse Muncey, a fisherman who had been employed in the building project, was appointed keeper "pro tem" with his salary set at $400 for an eight-month contract.

The original lighthouse was constructed of stone and was tapered from a twenty-one foot diameter at the base to eleven feet at the top. The tower stood forty feet tall to the parapet. In February 1833, a contract was made with Charles Morgan and Company in Connecticut to supply oil and maintain the lamps and equipment. Government regulations also required the keeper to be "*admonished from time to time of the importance of strict attention to their duty*" and reports to be made of any lack of oil or repairs during an annual inspection.

By July 1833, Muncey was appointed permanent keeper. Over the next ten years his reports have a persistent theme of structural problems, unreliable equipment and dwindling supplies.

In September 1833, Muncey sent a quarterly report to Abraham Wendell, Superintendent of Lights, including an inventory of articles on hand: tin butts, tin oil carrier, tin oil heater, iron stand, wick holders, cast iron stove pipe, lamps, reflectors, lantern, feeder, diamond, scissors, cleaners, glass panes, and a sixty-three gallon barrel of oil. This was also one of the first of many reports that would describe the precarious condition of the lighthouse:

The wite wash has washed of from the light hose soe thate the water passes threu the wall.

By this time, Muncey had obtained a boat for the lighthouse from Michael Douseman[2] who was leaving Thunder Bay after

[2] This appears to be the same Michael Douseman who had been taken prisoner by the British during their invasion of Mackinac Island in 1812.

being frustrated in his attempt to settle along the Thunder Bay River by Chief Michekewis. The lights were ended for the season on December eighth.

Over the next ten years, the lighthouse season generally followed the pattern of start-up in March, April, or May and closing in November or December. During an 1836 government audit, Muncey reported that he used about five quarts of oil per night. In a September report that year, Muncey detailed many complaints about the condition of lamps, lack of supplies, and leaks:

Sir I will give you a statement of the lamps in the lighthouse. The Inspector came to this place last fall and worked one day and part of one night and repaired two of the lamps and finally in the end broke two and left them in a worse situation than before.... I am now using two house lamps in place of them.... I have not enough to do me this Fall. And I have not received any wicks nor any tube glasses, no buff skin, no cotton, nor any whiting. I have received Nothing but the oil. The lighthouse leaks very bad.

He estimated that the fifteen to twenty barrels of lime needed to repair the leaks would cost $100. It was not only Muncey who was concerned with the precarious state of the station. Lieutenant James T. Homans detailed his findings in a November 1838 inspection report to the Fifth Auditor:

The buildings there are in a critical situation, and may, if not soon protected by some barrier, share the fate of one formerly near this site...undermined and destroyed by the action of gales on the lake.... The lighthouse is now nearly washed by the waters of the lake; should their present high state continue, it cannot stand long.... The best means of preservation occurring to me would be, to build cribs of large timber and fill them with stone.... Immediately in the rear of the present lighthouse buildings at this place is ground of considerably more elevation, where they would be safe; and it would, perhaps, be more economical in the end to demolish and rebuild them there.

In 1837, Abraham Wendell had confronted Muncey regarding the erratic nature of his required quarterly reports. In 1840, Muncey apologized with the excuse that bad weather had curtailed boat traffic. Nevertheless, in a July 1843 letter to Wendell regarding the condition of Thunder Bay Lighthouse and conduct of the keeper, a Mr. Wilson reported:

No repairs needed...Jesse Muncey is frequently absent for a fortnight at a time, leaving an old man in charge. Not inspected annually as required - not since 1840. Gave keeper notice that if he absents himself more than 24 hours without leave, his removal will be recommended. Must visit and report each year, without excuse.

Muncey's service did not last much longer. By December, he was replaced by a new keeper, William Terry. Terry's service was short lived. In the spring of 1845 he died, and in May the new keeper, J. J. Malden, reported the turnover of the lighthouse from William Terry's widow. Malden's approach to the job was more effective than Muncey, and he accomplished a number of critical repairs, procured a new boat and built a wood shed to be used in lieu of a badly leaking cellar.

But the structure was still in dire condition. In 1846, Malden reported that frost had caused heavy damage and leaks in the lighthouse. In January 1847, Malden was informed that there would be a new dwelling house constructed. He recommended that it should not be built of wood due to fire danger on the island (there had been fires the past two summers).

In May 1847, the lighthouse boat was stolen by two fishermen: Alonzo Nutting and Anson Hine. The boat was recovered ten days later – but both fishermen had drowned. By October 1847, the new dwelling house had been completed – "*very well built – far better than the first one*" according to Malden[3]. Even in the new dwelling, leaks were a problem, and in spring 1848, Malden stated that the solid limestone in the cellar was causing standing water of eight to twelve inches.

Malden requested help digging a drainage system and repairing plaster on the lighthouse, but over a year went by without any assistance. He finally appealed to the Collector, stating that he would do the repairs himself were it not for an injury he had sustained in a fall from the Saginaw lighthouse.

The most important duty of every lighthouse keeper was the care and operation of the lamp. The first lamp at Thunder Bay Island was most likely a "Lewis lamp array." This technology was developed in 1781 by Swiss scientist, Aime' Argand. It augmented a simple oil lamp's light by increasing combustion air to the wick with an induced draft system. This was later enhanced using parabolic reflectors and became very common in European lighthouses. In 1812, the Fifth Auditor, Stephen Pleasonton, introduced an American version of this lamp to the lighthouse system. It was named the Lewis Lamp by its maker, Winslow Lewis, and soon developed a reputation for poor reliability.

By 1852 the precarious condition of the nation's lighthouse system led to the establishment of the Lighthouse Board which would wrest control from the Fifth Auditor and provide leadership for the next fifty-eight years. The newly

[3] It is the author's belief that this was the detached, stone residence to the southwest of the lighthouse. It was demolished in the 1960's.

Lighthouse and Attached Keeper's Quarters in 1916 - prior to applying concrete coating in 1930's. Note the transition between the original stone tower (base) and the brickwork that was added in 1857 when the tower was raised in height. The year "1857" is just discernable on the brickwork below the lantern. (Photo courtesy of Central Michigan University - Clarke Historical Library)

formed Lighthouse Board appropriated improvements for Thunder Bay Island, and in 1857 the lighthouse was increased in height by ten feet. This was accomplished by wrapping the upper fourteen feet of the tower with brick and extending up to a new fifty-foot height at the parapet. This established the current sixty-three-foot focal plane above mean low water level. A new lantern was installed with a fourth-order Fresnel lens manufactured in Paris by Sautter. In 1822, Augustin Fresnel had perfected this type of lens, which was introduced to the U.S. in 1842 and ultimately became the standard for all U.S. lighthouses by 1859. These new lenses were very economical to operate, using only 1/4 the oil of the old Lewis array. This lens had six bulls-eye panels and a clock-powered turning mechanism. With these improvements, the range of the light was fourteen miles.

This is essentially the tower we find today, with a base that is 6'7" thick tapering to twenty inches at the top. Underneath a two-inch coating of sprayed Portland cement that was applied in 1938 (known as "shotcrete" or "gunite"), there is still the original smooth "Cream City" brick, which had been popular in the 1850's for the construction of many lighthouses.[4] The reason for this coating was to protect the degraded brickwork beneath. In 1917, George Putnam stated:

The outer brickwork of some of the earlier lighthouse towers erected on the Great Lakes has disintegrated to such an extent as to require repair... Recently the brick lighthouse at Evanston, Illinois Grossepoint has been repaired by covering the tower with concrete and cement mortar, over steel reinforcement.

Lighthouse complex - late 1800's. Note early fog signal building at right. Old keeper's quarters (1847) at left. (Photo courtesy of Ted Richardson Collection, Michigan Maritime Museum)

The "signal characteristic" of a lighthouse is the unique set of flashes and color that serves as its identity. In the 1861 Annual Lighthouse Board Report, Thunder Bay Island's light characteristic was described as flashing white every ninety seconds and visible for fourteen miles. In 1913, the characteristic was changed to a four-second flash, followed by a twenty-six second "eclipse." At this time the lamp was

[4] Until 1938, the color of the tower was described in various light lists as "yellow." After the cement was applied, the color was described as "gray." Today it is white.

converted from oil wick to oil vapor as an illuminant with an increase to 24,000 candlepower. The oil vapor lamp utilized a mantle instead of a wick. The first oil vapor lamps were installed in American lighthouses in 1904. According to Putnam, "*the kerosene, forced into the vaporizer by air pressure, is heated and vaporized and is burned mixed with air under a mantle which is brought to a brilliant incandescence.*" The range of the light was now sixteen miles. Later, by at least 1941, an electric light was installed and according to a 1953 light list, the period had been reduced to a four-second flash every fifteen seconds at 60,000 candlepower.

In 1868, the attached lighthouse keeper's house was constructed. It was two stories and about 2400 square feet. In 1867, the average lighthouse keeper's annual salary was fixed at $600. It was to remain at this level for the next fifty years.

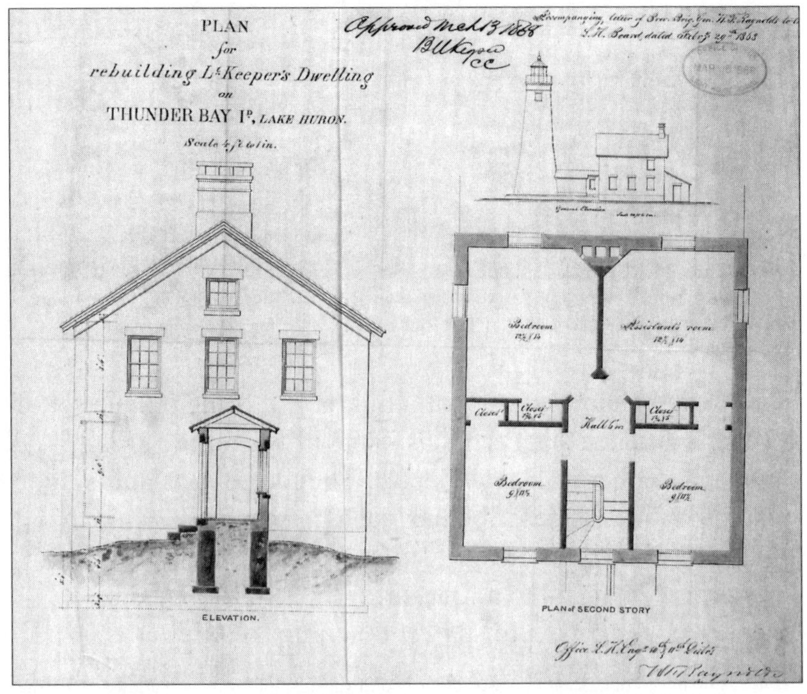

1868 Plan for Lighthouse Keeper's Quarters. (Courtesy of Walt Plohocky)

In 1852, the first foghorns and mechanically operated fog bells were being installed on the Great Lakes. In March 1855, a mechanized fog bell was installed just north of the lighthouse. However, an 1870 inspection report noted that the bell "*is not efficient for a position of its danger and importance*" and recommended a steam fog whistle. The following year, Thunder Bay Island had a ten-inch steam driven fog whistle installed in a wood-framed, metal-sided building. The fog whistle was driven by a horizontal locomotive engine. Unfortunately, it was not always reliable and the bell was kept for a back-up as described in a note from the 1876 Light List:

Should the steam whistle get out of repair, a fog bell struck by machinery will be sounded[5].

The characteristic of the whistle of this time was described as an eight-second blast followed by ten-seconds silence, then a

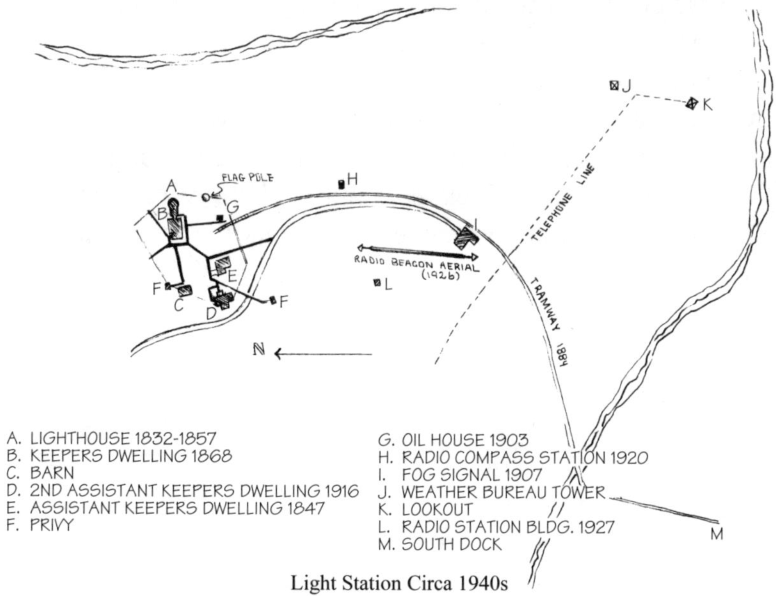

Light Station Circa 1940s

[5] According to a Lighthouse Digest article (July 1998), the bell was moved to Granite Island Lighthouse in 1879.

two-second blast followed by forty seconds silence. During an average season, the fog whistle operated 280 hours and consumed eighteen tons of coal. There were also occasions when the signal was utilized due to dense smoke from turn-of-the-century forest fires. Sometime between 1876 and 1884, a second fog signal house was constructed north of the original.

In 1884, an attached "stormhouse" and 1220 foot-long tramway were constructed. The tramway, used to deliver coal from the south dock, was destroyed by a storm in 1889 but rebuilt in 1891. The fog signal buildings were replaced in 1907 with the current brick building. In 1916, one of the old fog signal buildings was moved and converted to a residence for the 2nd Assistant Keeper.

In reviewing the lighthouse keeper's logbook from the 1890's and early 1900's one gets a glimpse of the daily routines. There are entries of wind and wave conditions as well as mundane tasks such as painting, cleaning, mowing, and maintaining the light and fog signals. There were also descriptions of visits from the mainland, working on the keeper's Mackinaw boat, hoisting storm signal flags, gathering wood and tending cows and chickens. Finally, there were supply visits from the lighthouse tenders including the *Amaranth, Marigold, Aspen* and *Lotus*. Here is a sampling from the 1897 logbook:

September 27 – Steamer St. Lawrence with disabled machinery, crew ashore to send word to owners. Getting winter's wood under cover.
October 1 – Went after a cow, cleaned signal whistles, getting up chicken feed from station.
October 3 – Considerable smoke from fire on mainland. Could not see North Point. Blowed whistle.

<u>October 5</u> – Keeper not well, got pain in his side.
<u>October 9</u> – Dorthea to town in Florence C to visit her folks. Keeper much better.
<u>October 13</u> – Working all day on Mackinaw boat. Put her in boat house for winter.
<u>October 17</u> – Tug Sarah Smith brought mail from town this morning. Clear pleasant day.
<u>October 23</u> – Fog 10:00 p.m. Blowed whistle 10:45 p.m. Steamer Tuscacora stranded about three hundred yards east of coal dock five minutes before the whistle started. Struck bottom at 10:40. Life Saving Crew to her assistance.
<u>October 25</u> – Little yacht Lotus of the Light House Engineers stranded on Kenosha reef between Sugar Island and the Mainland. Kept fire in Signal – threatening fog all day.
<u>October 28</u> – Blowing moderate gale tonight. Boats going in Thunder Bay for shelter.
<u>October 31</u> – Nothing of importance to day.
<u>November 5</u> – Splitting wood in afternoon. Southeast storm signals hoisted.
<u>November 6</u> – Blowed strong gale all day.
<u>November 24</u> – Butchered the bull. Cleaned ice house. Warmed up No. 2 Signal to keep from freezing.
<u>November 28</u> – Helped station crew to pull out Florence C.
<u>December 1</u> – Steamer Egyptian loaded with coal bound uplake burned up about 10 miles SSE of this station. Sturgeon Point Lifesaving Crew to her.
<u>December 8</u> – Forty five boats passed this island today. Remarkable fine weather for this time of year.
<u>December 11</u> – Laid up Whistle House No. 2 for the season.
<u>December 12</u> – Life Savers went out of commission today.
<u>December 19</u> – Ice forming around the island.
<u>December 24</u> – Having been satisfied no boats to pass this station this season, shut down the light and laid up Fog Signal No. 1. All in good order. Making ice fast in lake.
<u>December 26</u> – Had our Christmas dinner today. Captain,

Byron, Nina and Miss Richards here...had a very pleasant time.

Cement walks and a concrete cistern were installed in 1907. The cistern was meant to solve a common problem experienced by steam fog signals: the lack of reliable water supply. In October of 1897, it was cited as a possible cause of the steamer, *Tuscorora*, running aground on the southeast end of the island. From the Alpena *Argus:*

It has been claimed that the fog signals were not working on the island when the accident occurred, and this is not denied by Captain Persons.... Lighthouse keeper Cooney was using every effort to get steam and put the fog whistle in working order and no possible blame can be attached to the keeper.

In May 1900, when the steamer *H.D. Coffinberry* was wrecked at the island, the ship's captain was even more blunt in his criticism:

In regards to the fog whistle at Thunder Bay Island, the captain was not so loud in his praises. He says the government should see that the necessary means are furnished to keep the engine well supplied with water, and with the present method, in spite of all the keeper can do, the whistle often ceases altogether or is so faint that it sounds far off to boats near shore making captains think they are much farther out in the lake than they really are.

However, not until 1912 was a reliable water system installed. This consisted of a pipe line from the lake to the fog building cistern and then continuing on to the lighthouse cistern.

During the 1920's, the more reliable "Diaphone" foghorn technology was introduced at Thunder Bay Island, replacing the steam powered whistles with a compressed air system.[6] Steam had always been problematic for fog signals since it would take up to an hour to develop enough pressure for the whistle. In 1921, the "Type C" Diaphone was installed and then converted to a "Type F" in 1932. The two-tone characteristic of the signal was a pair of two-second blasts every thirty seconds.

As new navigation technology became available, it was introduced at the more critical locations such as Thunder Bay Island. The development of radio as an aid to navigation began in 1906 and was advanced by the Navy during World War I. Soon after the war it was implemented for civilian use. The systems fell into two categories: radio beacons and radio compass stations. By 1918, radio beacons were installed at all the major ports on the Atlantic seaboard, and in 1925 it was first utilized on the Great Lakes. Linwood Howeth described the operation of the radio beacon:

Vessels equipped with a radio compass detected the transmissions with the aid of a small loop mounted above a compass. The antenna could be moved in any direction. By listening with a headset, an operator rotated the antenna until the best (strongest) signal (from a radio beacon) was heard, then adjusted the frequency and took a bearing from another station. Plotting the directions of those signals on a chart, the point of intersection of those bearings is the ship's position. By listening to the characteristic signal each station was transmitting, it is possible to identify the station. There were many advantages to this new method of navigation, which was the forerunner of today's LORAN.

[6] For a detailed explanation of how the Diaphone worked, see Terry Pepper's website, "Seeing the Light."

In 1926, a 235-foot long radio beacon antenna was installed between two towers to the northwest of the fog signal building. The transmitting equipment for the beacon was in the fog signal building. It sounded a "dash-dot-dash" signal at a frequency of 286 kilocycles and was synchronized with the fog signal. With a simple computation, a ship could use the elapsed time between the radio beacon signal and the fog horn signal to calculate its distance from the island. John Floher described how this process was automated:

The radio beacon mechanism...consists of a transmitter which is thrown into operation by a master clock at specified times and interval. A small motor revolves a wheel, the periphery of which is divided into segments that correspond in length and number to the characteristic notes of the signal and that make electrical contact as they pass an electrode.

In addition, two areas were designated for use by the U.S. Navy Department as "Radio Station Buildings" between the lighthouse and fog signal. These were granted by the Secretary of Commerce to the U.S. Navy in September 1920. In 1919, the Navy Department had approved construction of ten "automatic wireless stations." The United States Lake Survey was assigned to determine locations for these stations.

According to <u>Charting the Inland Seas</u> by Arthur Woodford, a radio compass station was installed at Thunder Bay Island in 1920. Architectural drawings from March 1920 depict the design for a two-story radio compass building. The first floor included a living room and bunkroom, and the second floor was a smaller antenna room. The

Radio Compass Station (circa 1920). This was built by the Navy and used to locate vessels via the direction of an incoming radio signal. The tower contained the compass antenna.

radio compass served the opposite function of a beacon – that is, it was used to determine the direction of incoming radio signals from sources such as ships. The building appears in a 1920's photo of Thunder Bay Island, but it is not clear to what extent it was operated. A memo from the Navy Department Bureau of Engineering states that in 1923 *"as the Thunder Bay Island and Manistique Radio Compass Stations were then under construction and only partially completed, further construction was held up and these two stations were eventually abandoned."* A note on the drawing states that the building was *"turned over to L. H. Service 1927."*

Finally, a drawing exists of a "Radio Station Building" dated from September 1920 and, like the Radio Compass Building, designed by the U.S. Naval Training Station in Great Lakes, Illinois. This was a larger, two-story building with basement, office, dormitory, galley, dining room and living room. There was also a room for the "Electrician In Charge" and an "Operating and Receiving Room." The concrete foundation for this building still exists, hidden among the trees to the east of the old radio beacon antenna. It would appear that the building was never utilized due to a handwritten note on the drawing: *"July 1928. This bldg, rough floored, unplastered, roofed and 2/3 sided with all windows and exterior doors in place turned over to L. H. Service in 1927...."*

Ratio Station Building (circa 1928). This was built by the Navy for early ship-to-shore communications but apparently never used.

The Navy's involvement at Thunder Bay Island came to a close in 1930 when correspondence between the Secretary of Commerce and Secretary of Navy revoked the permits for this site and four others (including Detour Reef, Whitefish Point, Grand Marais and Eagle Harbor).

Aerial view of Lighthouse Complex in 1929. (Photo courtesy of U.S. Coast Guard Historian)

In 1939, the Lighthouse Board was dissolved and administration of navigational aids (lighthouses, buoys, etc.) was delegated to the Coast Guard. Chapter VII will provide details on the Coast Guard operation of the lighthouse. The Thunder Bay Island Lighthouse was automated in 1980 and, in 1984, placed on the National Historic Register.

While Thunder Bay Island's human history began with a lighthouse, the Thunder Bay region did not look promising at the conclusion of David Oliver's survey. As Oliver writes: "*It was conceded by the whole survey party, that the entire tract we had surveyed was worthless.*" With this, the group boarded a schooner and sailed off to Detroit. Little did Oliver realize that his travels would eventually bring him back to this "worthless tract" where he would figure prominently as a pioneer settler. He returned again in 1840 to survey Presque Isle and again in 1843 to trap and collect specimens for

Aerial view of Lighthouse Complex in 1962. (Photo courtesy of U.S. Coast Guard Historian)

natural history studies. In 1845, Oliver sold 109 marten pelts for $2.50 each, and with the proceeds he set up a store on Thunder Bay Island in 1846. The desolate island Oliver left in 1839 had been transformed into a lively fishing community with Oliver as one of its leaders.

List of Thunder Bay Island Lighthouse Keepers	
Jesse Muncey	1832-1843
William Terry	1843-1845
J.J. Malden	1845-1860
Daniel Carter	1860-1861
A.E. Persons	1861-1873
Patrick McGuire	1874-1882
John Sinclair Jr.	1882-1894
Michael M. Cooney	1894-1901
William R. Bennetts	1902-1919
Paul J. Klebba	1919-1928
Archebald Davidson	1929-1930
William DeRusha	1932-1939
Mathew Storback	1939-1941

CHAPTER IV – FISHING VILLAGE

"During the spawning season, the white fish in countless numbers swarm about the rocky bottom and hundreds of barrels of them get entangled in the gill nets."

- William Boulton, 1876 – describing Thunder Bay Island reef.

What drew David Oliver to try his hand at business on Thunder Bay Island was a prosperous fishing community established there by the 1840's. The story of fishing at Thunder Bay Island is filled with colorful characters. William Cullings was the first to fish from Thunder Bay Island as early as 1835. This coincided with what has been described by Margaret Bogue as *"the first period of notable growth of Great Lakes commercial fishing"* emanating from the "*expanding business community in Detroit.*"

"Uncle Bill" Cullings achieved legendary status during the early years of Alpena and Alcona counties. He was a true maverick. At age 26 he left a promising career as a schooner captain and sailed his Mackinaw fishing boat alone up the ninety miles from Port Huron to Thunder Bay. For the next sixty years he made a living as a nomadic fisherman and hunter. During this time, he is credited as the pioneer founder of Black River. Even the census taker of 1880 tried to capture the unique character of "Uncle Bill" when he listed his occupation as "ancient fisherman." R.E. Prescott had this to say about him:

Billy Cullings was a hardy man…men had to be tough-fibred to withstand the hardships of a frontier fisherman's calling, working in tiny open sailboats in all kinds of weather and living a primitive life wherever the vagaries of their nomadic life set them down.

In the 1840's, Cullings was joined by other fishermen including Harvey Harwood, Simeon Holden, William Hill and Robert McMullen. This group became a "who's who" of early Huron shore settlers. Harwood's fishery included a dock, fish house and cabins on the west side of the island in a small bay just north of the present boathouse. A 1996 archaeological survey by the Michigan State University Anthropology Department confirmed the location based on artifacts including ceramic and window fragments, barrel straps, clay pipes, bottles, nails, a silver spoon and pocketknife.

Simeon Holden had moved to Thunder Bay Island from Presque Isle with his wife, and his wife's sister and two children. He built the first frame building in the county on Thunder Bay Island in 1846. He would later become prominent in Alcona County as one of the founders of Harrisville, establishing a mill there with Crosier Davison in 1854.

William Hill was a character of heroic proportions and is credited with saving passengers from two early steamer wrecks near Thunder Bay Island: the *New Orleans* in 1849 and the *Ben Franklin* in 1850[7]. He was also the first settler of the village of Alcona, now a ghost town.

[7] In a letter to the Detroit *Free Press* (October 15, 1850) the wreck of the *Franklin* was described by lighthouse keeper J.J. Malden: "*Gents: with much regret I have to inform you of the total loss of the steamer Benj. Franklin at five o'clock yesterday morning on the shoal on the southeast point of the island. Passengers, officers and crew are all safe. By the prompt assistance of the fishermen with their boats…some 500 barrels of cargo is now on shore and most of the boat's furniture has been saved. The wind now is south and a very heavy sea running. The vessel is breaking up. I have been an eyewitness to what I stated. I was the first to board her after she struck.*"

Robert McMullen was noted as "*a Scotchman whose deeds of physical prowess and daring were legendary in the early days.*" Indeed, McMullen was credited "*with having pulled his new bride from Saginaw to his fishing camp here on a hand sled.*"

In 1846, there were thirty-one fishing boats and 160 people affiliated with the fishing operations at Thunder Bay Island. That season over 12,000 barrels of fish were harvested and shipped. The early fishermen used handmade gill nets with wood floats and stone sinkers. Fish were packed in salt and shipped down-lake in the fall.

Others had supporting roles to the fishing community. They included William Dagget and Washington Jay, who in 1844 were manufacturing staves for fish barrels at the mouth of the Thunder Bay River. Steamers had begun to call at the island in 1845, and by 1846 there was regularly scheduled service. According to David Oliver:

The fishermen on the island entered into an agreement with two steamers to call at the island every trip up and down during the season when the weather would permit and it became a habit with all the steamers when signaled for them to call, by hoisting a flag.

Paul Nelson Spoffard of New York City captured the flavor of this lively port in his journal of a voyage from Chicago to Detroit:

August 19, 1848. We stopped at Thunder Bay Island this morning. We soon had several boats around us to sell fish. They asked for a fine trout of 45 pounds only fifty cents.

For the next thirteen years, Thunder Bay Island was the "terminal" for all passenger boat traffic between Thunder Bay and the "outside world." Historian William Boulton explained that "*a person would be landed on Thunder Bay Island and then he would have to engage some fisherman to take him to Alpena by means of a sail boat.*"

In 1852, the first steamer entered Thunder Bay River, and by 1859 regular steamer service was being provided directly to Fremont (the first name given to the city of Alpena), bypassing the need for Thunder Bay Island as a waystation.

In 1854, Thomas Whelplen surveyed Thunder Bay, Sugar and Gull islands for the government. This provides a "snapshot" of the fisheries at the time. Harwood's fish house and dock were shown on the west central shore of the island, near the present Coast Guard boathouse. McDonald's fish house and dock were located on the east shore of Sugar Island. The 1850 census counted fifteen residents at the fishery including Mr. and Mrs. McDonald, their two sons, a cooper and nine fishermen. The 1854 survey also showed unnamed docks on the west shore of Sugar Island and at the future location of the Thunder Bay Island Life Saving Station. Also in the 1850's, a new type of net was introduced: the "pound net" which was designed to lead fish through a passage into a pot.

In the 1930's, R.E. Prescott interviewed fisherman Rufus Elmer of Harrisville and gave a description of Huron shore fishing during the 1850's:

Fish shanties dotted the sands, wooden reels turned and squeaked in the breeze, wooden net boxes and floats cluttered the shore and white and tan sails bobbed upon the waves...wooden poles with rags atop marked the beginning and end of the net lines beneath. Daylight saw the little sailing craft heading toward the buoys of the fishing grounds...Nets and hooks were set by ranges. Objects on shore were lined up, the first anchor stone dropped and the nets or hook lines set in a compass direction from that point. When storms blew out the buoys or markers, the starting point was found by the range and a grapnel dragged to locate the lines. Nets were made by hand, a wooden needle and a wooden mesh block being the tools used. Wooden floats were strung on one side of the net while lead sinkers were used at the bottom....Catches were cleaned, salted and packed in barrels and shipped "below" on schooners, and later on steamers which made trips frequently during the summer months.

John W. Paxton - Fisherman at Sugar Island during the 1860's and 1870's. (Photo courtesy of Central Michigan University - Clarke Historical Library)

The family name most closely associated with Thunder Bay's early fishing history was Paxton. Their story began in 1831 when John W. Paxton emigrated from England to America with his father, Peter Paxton. John W. and Peter first visited Thunder Bay Island in 1840 while sailing their 50-ton schooner, *Sparrow*. Over the next decade, John W. continued to "trade along the shore" of Lake Huron. In 1851, he was employed by Alpena pioneer David Oliver and became captain of Oliver's 75-ton schooner *Marshall Ney*. Paxton assisted in managing Oliver's lumber mill operation in Ossineke, as well as transporting finished product downlake to Cleveland. His sister, Sarah, had married David Oliver that same year. John W. was also married

Ann Whitten Paxton, wife of John W. Paxton of Sugar Island. (Photo courtesy of Rilla Whitten King)

that year to Ann Whitten, and they resided on Thunder Bay Island. In addition to his captain's job, John W. engaged in fishing from Thunder Bay Island. In 1856, he purchased his own schooner, the *Alpha*, and in 1858 was appointed Justice of the Peace for the island.

In 1859, Paxton placed a downpayment on nearby Sugar Island to W.H. Craig and moved his buildings and family there.[8] In the Michigan State University archaeological study, it was theorized that Paxton settled at the same location previously used by McDonald. He constructed new buildings including a cooper shop and fish packing plant. From Sugar Island, he operated a number of fishing boats including *Keystone* and *Dancing Feather*. He also operated a ferry service from Thunder Bay Island to Fremont. In the 1870 census, there were sixteen residents at the Paxton fishery including John W. & Ann, sons Charles & William, six fishermen, a domestic servant and four other family members. His son William took over the business in 1877, but it appears that John W. and his wife Ann continued to reside on Sugar Island until 1883 when they moved to Alpena. The Paxton "outfit" later expanded to include Charles Paxton and J.W. Troden as co-owners.

The Paxton name was even given to the bay between Thunder Bay Island and Sugar Island:

Paxton's Bay...is a good harbor for steamboats with 2-1/2 fathoms of water...It is worth the time spent to go in and examine this harbor. The lighthouse keeper or any of the fishermen are pilots amongst these islands. Mr. Paxton has a large fishing house here and good boat docks on each side of the bay.

Thompson's Coast Pilot - 1865

[8] This is according to Paxton's own journal. The Alpena County courthouse records indicate that Sugar Island was sold to W.H. Craig by Alexander McDonald for $2182 in April of 1860. The property was not officially sold to Paxton until April, 1863.

The Trelfa Collection at Central Michigan University's Clarke Historical Library has transcripts of John W. Paxton's Sugar Island journals from 1859 through 1874. Most of the entries are routine descriptions of the weather, daily tasks, and quantities of fish taken. Here is a sampling:

Friday, April 1st (1859).
Bought of W.H. Craig, the estate known as Sugar Island for the sum of sixteen hundred dollars, payable $500.00 down, the balance in two years, to take possession immediately, but subject to a limited base for one year.

Monday, April 11th
Took down my old frame of house to remove it to Sugar Island.

Over the next month, Paxton busied himself with building his cooper shop, fish house, breakwater and sleeping shanty.

Fishery at Sugar Island. (Photo courtesy of Rilla Whitten King)

Wednesday, May 25th
Set today and lifted, got about two barrels. Schooner Gem arrived, landed freight and shipped 16 half barrels and three barrels of fish... Father arrived and landed on his new home. May God prosper us.

And at the end of the season:

Wintered over 211 half barrels which sold in the spring at $8.75 per barrel for white fish. $7.75 for trout. Net proceeds $854.55.

William Boulton provided a further glimpse of the fishing industry that existed in the area during the 1870's:

Fishing is carried on by means of trap nets and gill nets. The trap net grounds are inside the bay, the best places being Campbell's fishery, Plough's fishery and Sulphur Island. The gill net grounds lie off the coast a distance of from five to ten miles. The number of rigs employed in fishing varies every year, but they number generally, about ten trap nets and ten or twelve gill net rigs. The yearly catch will average between four and five thousand barrels...the fish being packed in ice in Alpena and then shipped to various points below. The most convenient sites for the gill net boats are on North Point, Sugar Island and Gull Island.

The 1889 Lake Survey, conducted by the Bureau of Topographical Engineers, depicted six structures at the Paxton fishery. During a 1996 archaeological site survey by Michigan State University, there was substantial evidence of the fishery including lilacs, irises, an old apple tree and many artifacts including nails, glass, barrel straps, and clay pipe stems.

It is not known when the Paxton fishery ceased. The island was sold to Irvin Canfield in 1903 and by 1904, wreck reports located Troden's fishery on North Point. Wreck reports from 1912 and 1916 described the island as uninhabited.

A 1935 article in the Alcona *Herald* interviewed an early fisherman who reminisced about the "old days" and gave a "snapshot" of the fishing business around Thunder Bay during the 1870's. At the time, gill nets were being floated with cedar or bottle floats. Lead had replaced stone as the preferred sinker. Fish was salted and shipped in half barrels at a price of 2-1/2 cents per pound. In 1874, an attempt was made to utilize ice to ship fresh fish to markets in Detroit, but excessive spoilage ruined this enterprise. It would not be successful until later when faster boats were able to assure quick delivery.

The Whitten Family, fishermen at Sugar Island in 1891 - (left to right): Children Lucy, Guy, John, Frank, Ray and mother Rilla Whitten. (Photo courtesy of Rilla Whitten King)

The fisherman also recalled that the typical fishing "outfit" consisted of three crewmen on the boat, one man on shore to maintain equipment, and one cooper to manufacture barrels. There were two types of boats used: the "Double Cat" and the

“Mackinaw.” The Double Cat was 32-34 feet long with a foresail, mainsail and square stern. The Mackinaw was shorter and raked at both bow and stern. Thunder Bay was also noteworthy as home to the first steam fishing tug on the Great Lakes. According to John D. Persons (later Captain of the Life Saving Station), his father, A.E. Persons, built the tug *Lida* in 1875 which John D. (captain) and his brother Byron (engineer) operated from a dock on South Point.

In the 1880’s, the U.S. government established a fish hatchery in Alpena. This was precipitated by declines in the near-shore fish population due to habitat damage as a result of logging activities. A fisherman interviewed at the time summed it up this way:

Gone were the days when a sailboat and crew of four fishing eight to twelve nets caught 2000-3000 pound at one haul... now it takes a gang of sixty to eighty nets to catch as many pounds and it takes a steam tug and seven men to tend the nets.

At this time, fishermen made between $20-$35 per month, plus room and board. Boat captains could earn up to $100 per month.

By the turn of the century, Thunder Bay was second only to Saginaw Bay for fish production on the American side of Lake Huron. At this time, fish were routinely packed in ice that had been harvested from the Thunder Bay River and were shipped to markets as far as Detroit, Buffalo and New York.

An Alpena *News* article from 1926 stated that 2,500,000 pounds of fish had been shipped the previous year. Two hundred men were employed by the fishing business for ten months a year generating over one million dollar’s revenue.

There were ten large fishing operations (each with its own steam tug) and fifteen to twenty smaller operations (utilizing gas powered boats). The submarine/trap net, introduced at the turn of the century, had become very popular and effective. There were fishing operations in many locations throughout Thunder Bay including South Point, North Point, Whitefish Bay, Sugar Island and Crooked Island. The Alpena Fish Company was handling more than half of the annual catch. This included trout, whitefish, perch, chub, "finnies" and suckers. Refrigerator cars were shipping to Detroit, Chicago and New York.

However, by 1936 the Alpena *News* predicted trouble ahead for commercial fishing in the Great Lakes and blamed the deep water trap net for killing too many of the undersized fish. From 1940 to the 1960's, these predictions came true as the Lake Huron fish harvest declined from approximately 19% to only 4% of the overall Great Lakes catch. By the 1960's, after 130 years, the commercial fishing business in Thunder Bay was only a shadow of its glory days.

Nevertheless, the fishermen left a lasting legacy. As R.E. Prescott wrote in tribute:

Forced by their occupation to daily face danger and hardship, handling nets in storm and sunshine, water-soaked and half frozen as they worked barehanded in icy water, there was a reason for fishermen as a breed being classed as rough—only the roughest and toughest could stand the punishment. Living at the "edge of the world," the members of the fishing guild were the first permanent settlers.

CHAPTER V – LIFESAVERS

"My God, Captain, that lifeboat was the most welcome sight that terrible morning I ever saw in my life."

– Rescued schooner cook, October 1888.

Of all the stories of Thunder Bay Island, the lifesavers' are the most compelling. On April 18, 1936, a front-page obituary described the heroic life of Captain John D. Persons – "Hero of the Great Lakes." Persons epitomized the valor of the Life Saving Service and served as captain for thirty-eight years at Thunder Bay Island. This is the story of the Thunder Bay Island Life Saving Station.

Congress passed the Newell Act in 1848 to establish structures for housing life saving equipment along the shipwreck-prone New Jersey coast. However, it was not until 1871 that the U.S. Life Saving Service (USLSS) was established with Sumner Kimball, appointed by President Lincoln, as its General Superintendent. The driving force behind the USLSS was a terrible series of storms in 1870-1871 that resulted in massive loss of life and property. The USLSS was appropriated $100,000 and began its program on the Atlantic Coast. According to the Alpena *News*, by June 1874 Life Saving Stations were being appropriated for "*North Point, Presque Ile, 40-Mile Point and Sturgeon Point.*"

In September 1876, a station opened on Thunder Bay Island under Captain Issac S. Matthews. The same month, stations opened at Point Aux Barques, Sturgeon Point, Hammond Bay and Tawas. These were the first group of stations to open on Lake Huron. Matthews' command would last only one full season. In November 1877, Captain Neville of the schooner *Charles Hinckley* complained publicly that the lifesavers had neglected to provide aid to his boat when grounded at North Point. Matthews protested vehemently in the Alpena *Argus* of December 5, 1877:

Now the facts that the public should know that they may not unjustly cast blame where it is not deserved are these. I have at the station eight men besides myself, constituting one crew for the life boat... On the morning of the 8th, my wife and two men went to Alpena for provisions...and had got back as far as Campbell's fishery that night but the storm was so severe that they could not reach the station. In the morning they discerned the schooner "Empire State" and went to her aid. On the night of the 8th, I kept double watch and was up myself all night. In the morning, before breakfast, I discovered the "Sunnysides" and "Empire State" and at once started with the boat and all of the crew I had to their relief. The "Hinckley" could not be seen from the station as Sugar Island is between that station and the place where the "Hinckley" was stranded, which was about 600 yards from the shore and there was little or no sea running. After I had gone some distance on my course toward the "Sunnysides" I discovered on my starboard bow, the "Hinckley" and ran as close to the wind as I could towards her, but could not make her nearer than 100 yards, and hailed her. The captain replied, "We are all right and comfortable." I then went to Trodden's fishery and obtained three men and went to the "Sunnysides." After about two hours hard rowing we reached her and took her crew.

That night, Capt. Neville and crew cut their own boat from off the davits and went to Trodden's fishery, and from thence to

Alpena. The article misrepresents the station and the worthy men that worked hard that day. While the station did not render the "Hinckley" any assistance, it was because there were others whose conditions were worse than...the "Hinckley" and who needed help more... and anything that is intended to attach blame to the station is unjust in my opinion.

Issac S. Matthews
Capt in command Station No.4

Unfortunately for Capt. Matthews, his superiors did not agree with his defense. On December 19, 1877, the following appeared in the *Argus:*

We learn that Captain Issac Matthews has been removed from the Life Saving Station on Thunder Bay Island and that John D. Persons of this city has received the appointment as commander of the station to take immediate effect.[8]

Born in 1851 in Toledo, Ohio, John D. Persons had arrived in Thunder Bay on a schooner from Bay City with his father Alonzo (A.E.) in 1858. A.E. became a well-known pioneer and, in 1860, was elected the first representative from Alpena to the legislature in Lansing. In 1861, Alonzo was appointed lighthouse keeper at Thunder Bay Island, and in 1865 his fourteen year-old son, John, witnessed the tragic collision of the *Meteor* and *Pewabic* which resulted in the loss of over one hundred lives. This would leave a deep impression on him. Later in his career, after three previous salvagers had failed, John D. Persons helped Worden G. Smith of the American Wrecking and Salvage Company locate the *Pewabic.* An 1895 newspaper account described "*a novel experience*" associated with this salvage attempt:

[8] According to Frederick Stonehouse: "This is not surprising. Kimball did not tolerate any 'quibbling' or actions short of success."

The officers of the wrecker Root, which is working on the Pewabic a few miles from Thunder Bay Island, invited Capt. Persons and his guests to come out and watch operations. Capt. Persons and wife, Mr. and Mrs. Frank Case, Miss Nina Persons, Miss Clark and Ed Bishop went out and all enjoyed the novel experience of being lowered in the diving bell and viewing the famous wreck in 160 feet of water. The ladies exhibited no sign of fear and during their hour and a half's stay below were interested observers of the novel scene.

Years later, after retirement, Persons would recall the descent in Smith's diving bell as one of the highlights of his career:

I saw her lying on the bottom of the lake, 160 feet down.... The old Pewabic was a green ship lying in a bed of white sand. Ever see a water-soaked plank covered with green moss? Well, that was what the Pewabic was like.... We went from bow to stern and all around her in the diving bell.

By age 26, John was a ship-master and, with his father, operated the first steam fishing tug in Lake Huron, the *Lida.* It was Alpena banker George Maltz who recognized Persons' talents and character and recommended his appointment as captain of the Thunder Bay Island Life-Saving station. Persons fit the profile of the ideal candidate as articulated by Superintendent Kimball in 1912:

John D. Persons, Captain of Thunder Bay Island Lifesaving Station (1877-1915) (Photo courtesy of Ted Richardson Collection, Michigan Maritime Museum)

In the vicinity of nearly all stations there are a number who have followed their callings from boyhood and become expert in the handling of boats in broken water and among them there is usually someone who, by common consent, is recognized as a leader par excellence. He is the man it is desirable to obtain for keeper....

During the 44-year history of the USLSS, over 178,000 lives were credited as rescued (55,000 on the Great Lakes alone). A review of the station logs shows that Persons and his crews made their own contribution to this success story. In fact, Persons claimed that, under his leadership, over 1000 lives were rescued by the Thunder Bay Island crew.

A review of over 250 wreck reports from 1877 to 1916 reveals the following statistics:

The North Point reef was by far the most common location for wrecks, accounting for over 25%. Thunder Bay Island was a close second at 17% and Sugar Island at 6%. Not surprisingly, the most common cause of wreck was stranding (41%), followed by disabled engine (15%), leak/waterlogged (5%), and capsized (4%). The most common type of vessel assisted was the schooner or schooner barge (35%), followed by steamer/propeller (20%), fishing boat (11%), and tug (10%).

While assisting vessels in distress was the station's primary mission, the crew was also called upon for a variety of rescue assignments. Form 1807 – "Resuscitation of the Apparently Drowned" was filled out once by Captain Persons. The setting was a Sunday school picnic on Thunder Bay Island on August 11, 1892. The victim was a seven-year-old boy, Robert Clement, who was revived by artificial resuscitation.

As Captain Persons remarked:

A large Sabbath school picnic visited this island and station today and although every precaution was taken to prevent it, a boy fell off the dock. Just as he was sinking down, Keeper and Surfman Warwick ran as hard as they could and jumped into the (water) and got the boy, which had sunk to the bottom. Keeper placed his hand under his stomach and held him face down while getting him on to the dock. The water ran out of him and he soon caught his breath.

A newspaper reporter praised the crew:

Had the accident occurred almost anywhere else, the little fellow's life would have been lost; but in the hands of Capt. Persons and his crew, who know well how to handle such cases, his life was saved and he soon forgot that he had been so near death's door. Mrs. Persons clothed him in a complete new outfit of clothing from the Woman's National Relief stores... There is no safer place along the shores for children to enjoy a day's outing than at the life saving station....

The Thunder Bay Island Lifesaving Station was a popular place for visitors including church picnics and sports teams, like the Alpena YMCA football team shown here. (Photo courtesy of Jesse Besser Museum)

It was during this era of the Lifesavers that Thunder Bay Island became a popular destination from Alpena. In the 1890's, the Churchill Hotel included excursions in Mackinaw sailboats to the island as one of its attractions for summer visitors. A magazine article from 1882 described Thunder Bay Island as a *"favorite picnic ground of Alpena"* and recounted baseball games when mainland teams are *"over to tackle the station team, and the boys, strong from constant practice, always win."* Moreover, the station kept a pond of live sturgeon and *"visitors found fresh smoked sturgeon frequently on the bill of fare."*

This article from the Alpena *Argus* was typical for the 1890's:

An excursion was given to Thunder Bay Island last Sunday on the schooner Hunter Savidge which was patronized by about 200 people. A canvas roof was spread over the schooner's deck making her as pleasant an excursion boat as could be desired. She was towed by the tug Ralph and returned about nine o'clock in the evening. The trip was much enjoyed by those who went to the island.

Lifesaving crew prepared for beach apparatus drill. Captain Persons is at right. (Photo courtesy of Ted Richardson Collection, Michigan Maritime Museum)

Described as "The Flowery Isle" in a newspaper of the time, the Persons family took pride in attending to their gardens: "*Every trip over to the mainland the little steam yacht, Florence C., resembles a floral boat, it being loaded down with flowers for friends in the city. The variety and quality are not excelled.*"

There were other, more unusual outings to the island. While Captain Persons and his son often skated to and from the island during the winter, one March in 1917 (after his retirement) he set out with Fred Potter, Harry Garwod and John Richards in a Ford driven by the local Goodrich Tire dealer, Charles Steele. The newspaper described the event:

The trip was about 17 miles each way, four fifths of it on the ice. A little over two hours was required for the trip out...The visitors were made welcome by the Coast Guardsmen at the island. The automobile followed the tracks of sleighs, which have traveled between the island and mainland during the last two weeks. There was clear going most of the way, but an occasional stretch of jagged ice and snowbanks made progress slow. It was necessary to shovel snow several times when the car lodged in drifts.

The same month three men tried their hand at travelling to the island over ice on motorcycles. "*They don't intend to ever attempt the trip again,*" summed up the Alpena *News* article.

Horses, too, could depend on the life saving crew for assistance. Once, when a team was returning from cutting ice at the island, it was reported:

The ice gave way precipitating the team and men into the icy depths of cold Thunder Bay. The men put up a loud yell for assistance and were finally rescued, team and all, by help from the island, little the worse for their bath.

On many occasions, Captain Person's wife, Celia, became a vital, though unofficial, part of the team. She was the "quartermaster" of the supplies donated by the Woman's National Relief Association to clothe the victims of disaster. She cooked many meals and provided hospitality to the victims as well. Indeed, she was even apparently credited with saving a life. On September 13, 1907, the assistant lighthouse keeper's pregnant wife went into premature labor. It was dark and it was decided not to transport a doctor to the island. Captain Persons later related the story in a letter to the Superintendent of the Eleventh Life Saving District in Harbor Beach:

As soon as I got there I saw there was going to be all kinds of trouble in a few moments so I telephoned for Mrs. Persons at once and soon after she arrived this wife gave birth to a child. She had fallen and hurt herself and Mrs. Persons did every thing that could be done. In side of an hour the little woman was through her trouble and today is up and feeling well. As Mrs. Persons was the only one on the island that knew what to do under these circumstances....do you not think our service is entitled to a life saved....?

Described as "*a very quiet little lady, a graduate of Oberlin College and an accomplished musician,*" Celia E. Persons was also credited as the first woman granted captain's papers on the Great Lakes. Son, Byron H., and daughter, Nina, were tutored by their mother and later attributed success to the "*personal instruction which they received from their parents on the island.*" When Celia passed away in January of 1912, her obituary praised a life of service:

When the remains of Mrs. John D. Persons...were consigned to their last resting place in Evergreen cemetery Sunday afternoon, there was laid at rest one of the greatest life savers on the Great Lakes, and to the women of the service deep tribute is due. To hundreds of shipwrecked sailors she had administered. She fed, clothed and gave them succor. The blackest fireman, the ordinary deckhand and the master of a steamer all looked alike to her – human beings in distress. And to the thousands of visitors at Thunder Bay Island she was ever the genial hostess to make you welcome.

During this era, the shipping season generally ran from April to December and staffing of the Life Saving Station followed this seasonal pattern. The Persons family, however, lived there year-round. Indeed, the solitude was not unwelcome as Persons reminisced later:

There was one winter...a might cold one...when my wife and baby Nina and I were the only persons on that island. We had plenty to eat, lots of fuel and lots to read. It was a nice, quiet winter, just like being at the North Pole. All around, as far as we could see, it was white, desolate. I was reading about Peary and his North Pole exploration that winter, and it seemed to me we were up in the polar sea, too. There were ice hummocks around us 30 feet high in places. We were completely shut in. I can see it yet...our little home out in that white sea.

In 1912, an unusual request for assistance came from the distraught family of a young oiler from the steamer *Wyandotte*, Charles Cobo, who leapt off the ship while it was docked in an apparent suicide. Dragging and searching for two days, both the Alpena Police and Huron Cement employees were unsuccessful in locating his body. Captain Persons describes getting a call from the father:

He said to me, "Captain, if you will come over I know you

will find my boy." So there was nothing for me to do but go. I had steam made on my little steamer "Marcia," took a skiff and one man... Arriving at 11 a.m. I took charge of the work and by 2:30 p.m. we had recovered the body. Only those that have to perform these duties know how unpleasant it is, but it is very gratifying to feel that the people have such great confidence in members of the Life Saving Service.

The Life Saving Station itself was of the "Stick Style" design that architect J.L. Parkinson had utilized on many of the early stations. It cost approximately $5000 to build and equip. On the first floor were the boat house, kitchen, dining room and storage. On the second floor were the crew's and keeper's quarters. Finally, on the third floor was the lookout. The lookout was manned during daylight hours. Eventually, a lookout was constructed at the southeast corner of the island near the lighthouse. This provided a better view of shipping traffic and was eventually linked by phone to the station on the west side. In addition, the lifesaving crew rotated four-hour shifts for performing beach patrols. No day was complete without drills: boat drills, beach drills, signal drills and resuscitation drills.

Side view of old Lifesaving Station in the 1918. (Photo courtesy of U.S. Coast Guard Historian)

There is much written about the breeches buoy or "beach apparatus" (a device used to evacuate a vessel in distress using a line that was shot from land) and its importance in the Life Saving Service. This was apparently not the case at Thunder Bay Island. In over 250 wreck reports, there was none which mentioned its use. According to an article in the Alpena *Argus:*

Owing to the low shore in this vicinity, there is not much use for the breeches buoy as the crew can take the lifeboat to almost every vessel that gets ashore.

There were various ways that distressed vessels were discovered. In most cases, it was visual sightings of vessels flying distress signals or distress whistles alerting the on-duty surfman on patrol or in the lookout. However, the lighthouse keepers and local fishermen would also bring news of wrecks to the station.

On June 15, 1892, the Alpena *Argus* reported that $15,000 had been appropriated for the establishment of Weather Bureau[9] stations on Middle and Thunder Bay Islands and *"telegraphic communication between there and Alpena."*

This is an important matter to vesselmen, for now there is no such station between Old Mackinac and Port Huron and much loss of life and property will be saved by such stations as 40,000 vessels annually pass these points.

In 1893, telephone service was installed by the Weather Bureau and soon the station was receiving messages from Alpena, Middle Island, and North Point. This also allowed for

[9] The Weather Bureau had been established in 1870 as a branch of the Army Signal Corps. In 1890 it was transferred to the Department of Agriculture and evolved to the National Oceanic and Atmospheric Administration of today.

display of storm signals at the island. According to the *Argus:*

The telephone lines...proved of great value to navigation. On several occasions tugs summoned by telephone have arrived just in time to save a vessel, when if it had been necessary to have sent a boat to the city for a tug it would have been too late.

The most important equipment to the Thunder Bay Island lifesavers was the lifeboat. The standard lifeboat from 1876 through 1897 was designed by Captain J.H. Merryman and based on the traditional English lifeboat. It was constructed of wood and was 26' 8" long. It was self-bailing and self-righting and had a draft of twenty-one inches. There were three airtight compartments and three sails: the main, fore-mast and jib. These boats ranged in price from $500 to $1500. The first lifeboat at Thunder Bay Island, constructed in New York City by Stephen Roberts, was delivered in November 1876.

Persons had tremendous respect for these boats. In a 1902 correspondence to Superintendent Kimball, he calls it the "*perfect lifeboat*" and claims that the crew "*regard the boat as something almost supernatural.*" He states that it assisted in the rescues of fifty-three wrecks and "*she never failed to do her part, and to me she was like an old and tried friend.*"

In 1890, a big storm struck with particular fury on the south-east shore of Thunder Bay Island, destroying docks, buildings, and the boat basin. The lifeboat was so badly damaged that it was useless for any further service and was hauled into the woods with other damaged equipment. The remains of this boat are still on the island, and according to lifeboat expert William Wilkinson, it is one of only two remaining in the U.S. A new self-righting, self-bailing lifeboat was received by rail on October 28, 1891.

Original 1876 Lifeboat. (Photo courtesy of Jesse Besser Museum)

Thunder Bay Island also played "host" to one of the most historic of lifeboats. The *Valorous* had been exhibited at the 1876 Centennial Exposition in Philadelphia, and after many years in service at the Oswego station, was moved around to various stations including Thunder Bay Island before being retired to Hammond Bay in 1893.

In 1892, a new type of lifeboat was introduced at the Columbian Exposition in Chicago. It was thirty-four feet long and could hold as many as forty passengers. It was a sturdy boat constructed of oak and mahogany and weighed nearly 11,000 pounds. Thunder Bay Island had the distinction of being given the Columbian Exposition boat. It was delivered to the island in April 1894. Its arrival was hailed in the Alpena *Argus* on January 24, 1894:

The lifeboat that was exhibited by the government at the World's Fair was brought to this city last Wednesday and will be used next summer by the Thunder Bay Island Lifesaving crew.

Original 1876 lifeboat - damaged in 1890 and abandoned at the island. Retired Lifesaving Captain John D. Persons (left) and Coast Guard Captain E.G. Richardson (right). (Photo courtesy of Ted Richardson Collection, Michigan Maritime Museum)

A later article in the *Argus* continued the accolades:

The new life boat which was received this week for the Thunder Bay Island crew is certainly a beauty and one the crew may be well pleased to show their visitors...It is a perfect model and has been described by World's Fair writers as the finest life boat in the English services. It is 34 feet long and weighs 11,000 pounds and is said to have cost $5000 to build her. The keel is entirely of brass and she is fitted with two copper air chambers which run nearly her whole length. Her air valves are of copper and are set in even with the deck floor. The wood work is of the clearest mahogany which is not only durable but gives her a rich appearance.

It is evident that the officers have their eyes upon the Captain of the island station and know his needs pretty well. With this new boat, the boys can battle any kind of seas and can go anywhere duty may call them....Frequently the crew are called out for a ten or fifteen mile pull to answer some signal of distress and they are certainly entitled to the best that floats.

Columbian Exposition Lifeboat put into service at Thunder Bay Island in 1894. (Photo courtesy of Central Michigan University - Clarke Historical Library)

After some initial experiments in Marquette in 1899, the motorized lifeboat was introduced throughout the service at the turn of the century. They were typically powered by 35 to 40 horsepower motors and would remain the standard until 1961 when the Coast Guard introduced a new 44-foot motor lifeboat.

At Thunder Bay Island, the power lifeboat received its first mention in June, 1909 when the lifesavers used their 34-footer, named *Preserver*, to rescue the crew of the *W.P. Thiew.* In May 1910, *Preserver* received popular acclaim in the rescue of two injured men aboard the *Bulgaria.* The steamer was on a return trip from Buffalo to Ashland, Wisconsin with a load of coal. It was twenty-eight miles south of Thunder Bay Island – laboring in heavy seas off Sturgeon Point - when the main steam pipe burst, scalding two men. After temporary repairs were made, the *Bulgaria* steamed another eighteen miles flying a distress flag spotted by the Thunder Bay Island crew. They dispatched *Preserver* and arrived in a little over half-an-hour.

As Persons relates in the wreck report:

We soon decided to take the life boat and hasten to Alpena for doctors, with the steamer following slowly....We made all haste, secured two physicians and hastened back to the steamer, but one man died before we got back... everything was done for the other poor fellow that medical treatment could do.... We took the remains on shore and turned them over to the coroner....
Nothing was left undone by this crew that the Keeper could find to do to assist the disabled steamer and her crew. The power lifeboat demonstrated to the many onlookers in Alpena her great value at such a time....

The newspaper accounts of the day confirmed Captain Persons' assessment:

Drs. Secrist and McGuire were taken out to the Bulgaria. When the lifeboat arrived, James Burns was dead from the

36-foot Motor Lifeboat at Thunder Bay Island. (Photo courtesy of Jesse Besser Museum)

terrible scalding he received. The surgeons dressed Frank Cassidy's injuries and he was brought here on the life boat and taken to J.R. McDonald's boarding house where late this afternoon the surgeons gave the man more extended attention... His face and hands are badly scalded and it is feared he inhaled some of the steam....Where the pipe burst the terrific force of the steam blew a hole in a steel plate.

"Preserver" does not belie its name. The value of the power life boat at the Thunder Bay Island life saving station was more than demonstrated Tuesday and too much praise cannot be given the "Preserver," the appropriate name of the life boat....It is the real thing in life saving apparatus and the life savers are proud of her.

Besides the lifeboat, lifesavers depended on a lightweight surfboat for shorter trips. It was made of cedar and ranged from 25 to 27-feet in length. It could hold up to fifteen passengers and weighed between 700-1000 pounds. Costing

Surfboat drill at the Coast Guard station. (Photo courtesy of Ted Richardson Collection, Michigan Maritime Museum)

only about $300, the surfboat was maneuvered using a steering oar. It had first been developed on the coast of New Jersey before its introduction throughout the Life Saving Service.

The earliest surfboat at Thunder Bay Island was a square stern Jersey boat, but by 1895 a Beebe-McLellan design had come into use. This was a double ended, self-bailing model with some enhancements over the Jersey boat. The Jersey boat was kept and did provide some occasional assistance in later rescues when needed.

Surfboat house - located at Coast Guard station - 1930. (Photo courtesy of U.S. Coast Guard Historian)

The Thunder Bay Island Life Saving Station was aided by another vessel, the *Florence C*. This was Persons' own four-ton, 28-foot wooden steamboat mentioned in wreck reports

Postcard of Thunder Bay Island Lifesaving Station circa 1890. Note original lifeboat in background and captain Persons' steamboat, Florence C, in the foreground. (Photo courtesy of Ted Richardson Collection, Michigan Maritime Museum)

beginning in 1891 through 1909. The *Florence C* was constructed in 1889 at Thunder Bay Island. The engine had been donated to Persons by local residents in appreciation of his service assisting five ships during a terrific storm of October 2, 1888:

The vessel owners in the city of Alpena, realizing the need of a more rapid transit between the island and the city, and also as a token of their esteem and appreciation of his labor, presented the captain with a complete steam outfit for his new yacht, the Florence C, a very staunch craft, built of the best material and able to weather a very heavy sea. She runs from the island to Alpena in about one and one-half hours.

A newspaper account from 1892 further described the *Florence C:*

She has a small deck fore and aft and her cabin extends the full width of the boat. Besides the pilot house, the cabin is 8 feet square and the engine and boiler room give ample room for two men to work and her coal bunkers carry a supply of fuel to run 24 hours. She has an engine, 5 x 4-1/2 , devel-

oping a speed of ten miles an hour....The Florence C will carry 15 to 20 people comfortably and is used in taking supplies to Thunder Bay Island... She is also a great convenience in bringing word of marine accidents to port and securing the assistance of tugs, thus enabling tugs to get to the distressed vessels several hours sooner than if the surf boat had to be sent in as formerly. The use of the steamer also leaves the surfmen free to aid distressed vessels.

At the time of this article, the boat had been lengthened to forty feet. Celia Persons was listed as Captain of the boat and Surfman Warwick was acting as Second Engineer.

The Florence C, after it was lengthened in 1891. (Photo courtesy of Jesse Besser Museum)

In 1910, the *Marcia*, referred to as the "keeper's steam yacht," was receiving mention in wreck reports as assisting in rescues. The 44-foot-long *Marcia*, which replaced the *Florence C*, was constructed of oak with an 11-foot beam and was equipped with a 25-horsepower boiler which powered her at twelve miles per hour. The *Marcia* was also constructed at the island, with the help of the surfmen.

One other group of vessels deserves mention in their supporting role to the Life Saving Service: the local tugboats that assisted with lightening loads, pulling stranded vessels free, and towing to port. Of all the tugs, the one mentioned most often was the *Ralph*. The 42-ton tug *Ralph* was originally built in 1874 as the *E.H. Miller* and was 60 feet long with a 15-foot beam. In 1875, while racing another tug in the quest for a tow, the boiler exploded sending it to the bottom off North Point, and killing Captain Edward Miller and the cook, William Moody. It was bought and raised by J.D. McDonald and by 1880 was back in service with a new engine. In 1883, Gilchrist and Fletcher bought the tug, lengthened it by four feet and renamed it the *Ralph*. The *Ralph* provided faithful service to the port and lifesavers for the next 34 years until 1917 when it burned. It was sunk off the pier at the end of Chisholm Street.

Tug Ralph which assisted in many shipwrecks between 1883 until it burned and sank in 1917. (Photo courtesy of Jesse Besser Museum)

No matter how well equipped a station might be, it was only as effective as the men who served it and put their lives on the line. While there was much glamour associated with the jobs of keeper and surfman, there was not much pay for such hazardous occupations. In the early years, pay for keepers averaged around $400 per year and for surfmen it was $40 per month. A portion of this pay went for meals. Some stations would hire a cook. Others might rotate the food preparation duties among the men. There were examples of both at Thunder Bay Island.

Most life saving stations had a keeper and eight surfmen. The men shared camaraderie and pride in their team. One of the island's treasures is a rock proudly carved in 1879 with the names of Persons and his eight surfmen: McKenzie, LeClair, Russel, Steele, J.K. Persons, Teno, Lenord, and Ferris.

Some of the men who served under Persons at Thunder Bay Island went on to have notable careers in the Coast Guard.[10] J.D. Plough, who retired as Captain from the Port Huron Life Saving Station in 1915, had served on one of the first life-saving crews at Thunder Bay Island.

H.D. (Harry) Ferris, who had been selected by Persons in 1878 as surfman and was previously a fisherman in Thunder Bay, went on to become Captain of lifesaving stations at Pointe Aux Barques and Harbor (Sand) Beach. He was on duty up to the age of 81 and finally retired at the conclusion of his 41-year Coast Guard career.

Another notable was Fred Poirier, whose 30-year Coast Guard career also began at Thunder Bay Island under the leadership of Persons. He was stationed there from 1899 until 1926 when he was transferred to Sturgeon Point and eventually promoted to Captain in 1928. During reminiscences at his retirement in 1929, Poirier recalled bringing *"supplies to the station from North Point over the ice by sleigh, driving a*

[10] From a booklet published by the Ninth District U.S. Coast Guard for its 1932 annual picnic: "*The two island stations of the Ninth District have made history...These two stations, Thunder Bay Island and Middle Island, have been the training school for many of our present officers in charge.*"

team." He also shared vivid memories of storms in 1910 and 1913 that resulted in the wrecks of steamers *Blanchard* and *Arcadia.*

Finally, Eugene Motley, who served under Persons as surfman, went on to become Captain at Middle Island.

The life saving crew experienced its own tragedy in 1911. On the morning of October 31, 35-year-old surfman Adolph Schroeder and Assistant Lighthouse Keeper Charles Robbins were on a run between Alpena and the island. They were both returning from shore leave. A "nor-easter" blew off the lake and caused the rigging to fail just three miles from the island. Robbins related the tragedy first hand:

The outhaul on the mainsail at the end of the main boom gave way. I made the repairs. At the time we stood well off into the lake, outside of the can buoy. We then put the boat in stays. As she was going around, the outhaul gave away again. Schroeder was steering. He said "Charley, you take the stick and I will fix that." I immediately took the stick, looking to see if the foresail had a good full on, when something startled me. I looked around and saw Schroeder pitch head-first into the lake.
My first thought was a line to throw him. But nothing being

Captain Person's "water and ice punt" which allowed for winter travel between the island and mainland before the ice was solid. It was built by surfman Elias Knudson during the 1890's. (Photo courtesy of Jesse Besser Museum)

available I got a life belt out of the locker and threw it as near him as I could. He was by this time some little distance from the boat. I then turned the boat around as soon as possible. In going around the mainsail cock billed, putting the boat in a bad condition to handle. Schroeder was then swimming close to the lifebelt. I looked up at the sails, then looked again and he had sunk down. This all occurred, I think, in less than five minutes. During this time I was frantic to see my friend being slowly dragged under the water with his heavy clothing.

Meanwhile, the lifesaving crew and Persons family were watching the boat, but aside from concern about the rough weather, they had no indication of the disaster that was taking place. An hour later, they received a call from the Troden fishery at North Point. The power lifeboat was manned and a search commenced, but Schroeder was never found.

In Persons' November 1, 1911 report to Superintendent Kimball, he related the mood on the island:

To say that I and every person connected with this station was stunned would be putting it very mildly... The service can ill afford to loose such surfmen as Adolph Schroeder. It is another case of a good and faithful man sacrificing himself to the Life Saving Service.

In an Alpena *News* article, Persons was quoted:

He was one of the best men I ever had... we are all prostrated over here. I have never had anything so upset me since I have been in the service.

Superintendent Kimball ordered the Assistant Inspector of the 10th and 11th Districts in Detroit to make an investigation and secure sworn testimony in regards to the casualty. He wanted an opinion as to *"whether the accident occurred within the scope of the Service."* The following summer a report was forwarded to Kimball by Assistant Inspector Capt. Lewis. It contained the testimonies of Capt. Persons, surfman Edgar Brown and Assistant Lighthouse Keeper Robbins, and it exonerated the Life Saving Crew in regards to the incident:

As no signal of distress was hoisted and the distance from the life-saving station was too great to discern even with the aid of marine glasses that a man had fallen overboard, the casualty was clearly not within the scope of the lifesaving service, and no blame can be attached to the Thunder Bay Life-Saving Crew.

Another low point was when a life saving crew, at the end of the 1897 season, leveled charges against Capt. Persons for neglect of duty. Two specific incidents were cited where Persons chose not to respond to an apparent vessel in distress – the *Miami* on October 24 and the *Egyptian* on December 1. Supt. Kimball assigned a Lieutenant Reinburg to the case and his investigation took place at the Churchill House in Alpena. After hearing testimony from all involved, Reinburg reported his findings to Kimball. On March 18, 1898, Kimball deliv-

Egyptian (Photo courtesy of Labadie Collection - Thunder Bay Sanctuary Research. Collection, Alpena County Library)

ered his verdict from Washington, D.C.:

Keeper Persons was charged with neglecting to respond to signals of the Miami...and failing to go to the aid of the Egyptian....Captain claimed Miami signals were not for assistance and no aid from the life saving service was needed by the Egyptian. He could see vessels standing by Egyptian.[11] *No adverse results ensued, but department holds he should have gone out in both instances. All doubts must be resolved in favor of action. Captain Persons is censured, but in view of his long, able and meritorious services no further action is now contemplated.*

S.I. Kimball

With this, the Alpena *Pioneer* reported:

Capt. Persons' many friends will be pleased to learn the result of the investigation. The charges were very grave and had these charges been made against almost any other officer he would almost certainly have been dismissed.... Capt. Persons' long and able service are evidently appreciated by the Department, and The Pioneer with all Alpena citizens will be pleased that he is to remain in charge of the island.

Persons remained in active duty until 1915 when he retired. At the time he was 64 years old and the oldest keeper on the Great Lakes. This was at a time when the maximum age for the appointment of a new keeper was 45 years. This was also the year that the Life Saving Service was combined with the U.S. Revenue Cutter Service to become the U.S. Coast

[11] Captain Persons assessment of the *Egyptian* situation turned out to be accurate. The *Egyptian* had caught fire about half-way between the Thunder Bay Island and Sturgeon Point Lifesaving Stations. The Sturgeon Point crew, under Captain Henderson, rowed three hours to reach the vessel which was about fifteen miles from the station, only to find that the ship was empty since the crew had been taken off by the steamer *Fairbairn* some time before. Having burned to the water line, it was a total wreck and sank in 170 feet of water.

Guard.

There were a number of reasons leading to the decision for this merger. The Life Saving Service was faced with some harsh realities. First, the Service and equipment had been designed and implemented at a time when the majority of ships were sail-driven. With the ascent of steam-driven ships and recreational gas-powered boats, the Life Saving Service was less effective in its rescue abilities. Secondly, the many years of sub-standard pay had made recruitment efforts for young surfmen and keepers difficult. As Dennis Noble explains:

Salaries became too low to attract new men and, with no retirement, it became difficult to gain promotion. By 1914 there were instances of keepers in their seventies manning the customary sweep oar while the strokes were manned by men in their sixties. In 1914, after years of trying to obtain a retirement system, Kimball agreed that a merger of the U.S. Revenue Cutter System and the U.S. Life-Saving Service would be best for both services and the country.

Persons was typical of elderly lifesavers who were able to pass their annual medical exam and dodge efforts to set a mandatory retirement age of sixty. The cynical Lt. McLellan wrote in 1899:

The fact of them passing the medical exam does not make them fit to do the work of the service; in fact some of them will pass the medical officer until they dry up and blow away.

Nevertheless, there is no such cynicism in any of the newspaper articles that lauded Persons after his retirement, and Persons was clearly ambivalent about his prospects:

I'd rather wear out than rust out...There are other men in the service who are not as physically fit as I seem to be and I would rather see them given a rest than myself....I suppose it will be all right after I adjust myself to the new order of things, but I can't say that I like to give up my snug little home at the island. I hate to give up my little garden. My only satisfaction is that I will remain on call for special duty and in an emergency I will have a chance to get back to the island.

Suffice to say he ended his years with the respect that comes from proven heroism and sacrifice. After Persons retired, he remained a central figure in Alpena until his death in 1936. His obituary lauded him as "*Alpena's Grand Old Man*" and "*raconteur of rare ability – hunter, fisherman and genial citizen, beloved and respected by all during a residence of more than 7 years.*"

The good old captain seemed to have captured something of the spirit of eternal youth. Some of the secret may be indicated in the fact that people never heard him speak unkindly to others. In his eighties, he could laugh like a boy of twenty; in the last year of his life he was still a good hunting and fishing companion for people a third his years. He had discovered a secret of life that many men the world may call wiser, would like to know.

While the Life Saving Service disappeared, it's legacy endured. Dennis Noble wrote:

The United States Coast Guard, building upon the strong foundation established by the U.S. Life-Saving Service, and adding its own efforts, has become the recognized expert in search and rescue over the water. The development of the 36 and 44-foot motor lifeboats, the establishment of a search and rescue school, and the use of the helicopters have increased the U.S. Coast Guard's reputation as the leading agency for those "in peril upon the seas."

Today, the men and women of the U.S. Coast Guard carry on the traditions of service to others established by the crews of the U.S. Life-Saving Service; but with more sophisticated equipment, they are able to surpass the records of their illustrious predecessor.

Captain Persons' own scrapbook contained this newspaper clipping titled "All Honor to the Life-Savers," which summed-up his own career pretty well:

Remote from the centers of population, these brave men lead lonely and dreary lives, save when some unfortunate vessel is driven upon the neighboring coast...it reminds the country that it has no more valiant and valuable band of servants than the life saving crews. All honor to these fearless saviors of human life.

CHAPTER VI – SHIPWRECKS

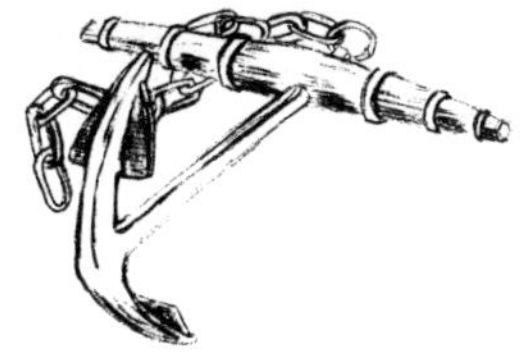

In 2000, the National Oceanic and Atmospheric Administration declared Thunder Bay a National Marine Sanctuary. Its focus would be underwater archaeology – most notably the shipwrecks that litter the bay and surrounding coastline. The great concentration of shipwrecks in this area was a result of two factors – the shallow, rocky, treacherous waters and the high density of shipping traffic that funneled by Thunder Bay.

The history of Thunder Bay Island is interwoven with the history of shipwrecks. While ships had been plying the waters of Lake Huron since the *Griffin* first sailed in the 1600's, the shipping industry came into its own during the 1800's. This resulted from a combination of factors: steamboats, which first appeared in 1817, the Erie and Welland canals in the 1820's, the rise of copper and iron mining in the 1840's, and the opening of the Soo Canal in 1855. In 1869, sailing ships reached their zenith and then were eclipsed by the steamers, including the first iron-hulled ships in the 1880's and the first self-unloaders at the turn of the century.

Along with the rise of shipping in the Great Lakes, a navigational infrastructure was needed – and in this regard the island played a prominent role in providing a lighthouse (1832) and life saving station (1877). Other equally important maritime safety improvements included the first light beacon ships in 1841, the 1859 Lake Huron survey, and navigation "rules of the road" in 1864. In 1870, a marine weather service was begun. Even with all of these advances, there were still many hazards associated with lake travel, as can be seen by reviewing the wreck reports of the Thunder Bay Island Life Saving Station from the late 1800's and early 1900's.

There are over 250 wreck reports on file for the lifesaving station during Captain Persons' tenure. Each rescue posed unique challenges to the crew. Here is a sampling of them:

<u>October 4, 1883 – James Davidson and Middlesex</u>

Some wrecks deposited themselves at the "doorstep" of Thunder Bay Island. One of the most dramatic was the steamer *James Davidson* bound for Duluth from Buffalo with a load of coal and a crew of eighteen men. Towed behind the *Davidson* was the 500-ton schooner-barge *Middlesex* with a crew of eight. At about 10:00 p.m. on the night of October 4, 1883, the lifesaving crew heard the whistle of the *Davidson* being blown in distress. Within fifteen minutes, the crew had hustled the half-mile across and was on the scene at the southeast end of the island. The two vessels were found side-by-side about 400 yards from shore. They were grounded and the sea was causing them to beat one another to pieces. The lifesavers went quickly to work, shifting the cargo on the *Middlesex* aft to try to float her. By morning, a steam tug, the *Swain*, was on the scene and pulled the *Middlesex* out of danger. The *Davidson*, on the other hand, was a total loss and had sunk.[12] In his report, Captain Persons blamed the wreck on swift currents drawing the *Davidson* off course. The Alpena *Argus* told the story:

It appears to be just as difficult for a large vessel to run over Thunder Bay Island as it is for a small one and the propeller Davidson found it to be so. That boat not only undertook to sail over the island, but she tried also to tow the barge

[12] The remains of the Davidson were not identified until the summer of 2003 when divers found them off the south end of the island.

Middlesex over the same place. The Jas Davidson is a large double decker and had on board 1500 tons of stove coal and about 200 tons of soft coal. On Thursday night she got to Thunder Bay Island sooner than was calculated and run hard aground near the lighthouse... About one to two hundred tons of coal were dumped off the Davidson, but it proved of no use and a dispatch was sent to Detroit for a diver and pumps... During Friday night the Davidson lay on the rocks exposed to heavy sea and received severe damage. On Sunday the tug Winslow arrived with two pumps, diver and other wrecking apparatus...The Davidson was exposed to another heavy sea Monday night and there is not much prospect of saving her.

After convincing the captain of the Davidson to abandon ship, *"Ten men were taken into the life-boat and four each put in the steamer's two yawls. The yawls were then taken in tow, and by keeping outside the surf until behind the island, a landing was made on the lee side without much trouble. The people were all made as comfortable as possible at the station...On the following days, the station crew took advantage of every opportunity in saving all that was possible from the steamer...The vessel became a total wreck, and but a small portion of her cargo was recovered."*

Annual Report of the U.S. Life Saving Service, 1883

October 2, 1888 – Dan Rogers, F.B. Gardner, Chester B. Jones, Manitowoc, Susquehanna

One of the most memorable storms that ever swept Thunder Bay occurred in October 1888. The northeast gale resulted in the wrecks of four schooners and a steamer. No single storm tested the life saving crew at Thunder Bay Island more than this one. The following account is excerpted from the Annual Report of the U.S. Life Saving Service for 1888.

The night was one of great anxiety and alarm to the life savers of Thunder Bay Island... The in-rushing surf submerged the northeast end of the island...and there was every prospect of numerous disasters to exposed vessels... Few of the life-savers rested that night; they kept on their cork jackets ready for a call and maintained a watch along the shore.

Captain John D. Persons described the efforts of the life-savers of Thunder Bay Island that day:

At daylight, four schooners were to be seen from this station flying flags of distress, two of them at anchor exposed to the full sweep of the sea and gale and two on the North Point reef. One of the vessels was nearly torn in pieces, booms and gaffs hanging over the side, canvas blown away, full of water and badly listing.

The life saving crew sailed and rowed, providing assistance in succession to each vessel: the water-logged barge, *Dan Rogers*; the schooner, *F.B. Gardner* which had lost its sails; the leaking schooner, *Chester B. Jones,* and the *Manitowoc,* which had lost its rudder.

All of these vessels were loaded with lumber, hailed from Buffalo, New York and had crews of seven. They were spread over an area of three miles. Meanwhile, Celia Persons watched anxiously from the station. She later stated that *"...when the life-boat descended into the trough of the sea, it disappeared entirely from her view."*

The life saving crew next set sail to Alpena for assistance.

The steamer, *Garden City,* and the tug, *Ralph,* were on their way by 10:00 a.m. Before the day was over, however, they would provide aid to yet a fifth vessel: the steamer, *Susquehanna,* which found shelter in Alpena after a torturous trip of seventy-five miles after losing its rudder off Pointe aux Barques. The Alpena *Pioneer* praised the lifesavers:

The test was severe upon their skill and endurance, but they succeeded, thereby saving a number of lives and many thousands of dollars' worth of property... Keeper Persons and his life-saving crew deserve the greatest praise for their exertions.

November 28, 1904 — B.W. Blanchard, John T. Johnson, John Kilderhouse

Today if you venture out with snorkel and mask to the shoals off North Point, you will see wreckage strewn over an area about the size of a football field. An anchor, a windlass, some curved beams and other debris are all that remain of two ships that were stranded there during a southeast gale that ravaged Lake Huron one November night.

B.W. Blanchard. (Photo courtesy of Labadie Collection - Thunder Bay Sanctuary Research Collection, Alpena County Library)

The *Blanchard* was a 34-year-old, 526-ton steam package freighter hailing from Detroit. It was southbound with 700,000 feet of lumber from Cheboygan when it encountered a terrible snow and windstorm. The *Blanchard* was also towing two schooner barges: the *John T. Johnson* from Cheboygan and the *John Kilderhouse* from Detroit. They each carried an additional 600,000 feet of lumber.

The gale began blowing late that afternoon and was building through the evening. When the boats reached Thunder Bay, the decision was made to run into the bay for shelter. However, by about 10:30 p.m., the southeast wind blew them onto the rocks.

At 11:45 p.m., torches were sighted on North Point by the No. 1 surfman who alerted Captain Persons. The crew was readied, but Persons hesitated:

When I went out on the dock and saw the way the breakers were running I knew I could not go to the windward of Sugar Island, and to go the other way among the reefs in the darkness and snow would be a dangerous risk too great to take.... My better judgment told me to wait for daylight. I stayed on the beach and kept close watch until four o'clock, then had a

Wreck of the B.W. Blanchard off North Point in November, 1904. (Photo courtesy of Labadie Collection - Thunder Bay Sanctuary Research Collection, Alpena County Library)

cup of coffee and went up and launched the lifeboat. At daylight we were in heavy breakers on the south side of Sugar Island and saw wreckage. So with sail and oars made all haste we could... We went right out to the steamer which I saw was breaking up... but there was no one on board.

The thirteen crewmembers of the *Blanchard* had abandoned ship around 4:00 a.m. In an Alpena *News* article, one crewman related the story:

The wind pounded the boat against the rocks and in a short time her timbers began to loosen. The load began slipping away and as the sides of the boat gave way, the lumber in the hold began to clear. We remained on the boat until 4 o'clock and had to take to the yawl to save ourselves. We left none too soon as the boat was a complete wreck a few minutes later.

Persons would later question the judgement of the *Blanchard's* captain:

Nothing but a miracle saved their lives. I asked the Captain the next day why he did it and he said "I did not think it was possible for you to get to us and we took what we thought was our only chance." ... If this crew had held on until a little after daylight, we would have taken them off.

It was now about 7:00 a.m., and the lifesaving crew pushed on to the *John T. Johnson*.

She was broken in two, her main mast over board and deck-load mostly gone... a total wreck. Her crew was soaked with water, very cold and in bad shape – they had put in a terrible night of suffering. I took them off and landed them at Troden's fishery.

After landing the seven crewmembers of the *Johnson*, it was on to the *Kilderhouse*. When they arrived a little after 9:00 a.m., they found an exhausted crew that had not only fought a storm all night but also had two fires break out in their cabin. They were also landed at Troden's. The tug *Ralph* took both crews back to Alpena, but there was still unfinished business:

The cook had a large trunk full of clothes and the captain said it was all the poor girl had in the world. So I took it in the lifeboat. She called me the next day and thanked me for my kindness.

Over the next few days, the crew would assist in removing cargo, transporting the owners, and running lines. The *Johnson* and *Blanchard* were total losses. But by December 16, 1904, the Reid Wrecking Company had managed to remove the *Kilderhouse* from the rocks.

<u>November 23, 1907 – Monohansett</u>

While waiting out some heavy weather near Thunder Bay Island on its journey from Cleveland to Collingswood, Ontario, the *Monohansett*'s crew had the good fortune of being only a short distance from the Lifesaving Station when fire broke out. Carelessness with an engine-room torch in an old wooden vessel was the cause, and in only a few minutes the entire stern section of the boat was engulfed in flames.

Monohansett (Photo courtesy of Labadie Collection - Thunder Bay Sanctuary Research Collection, Alpena County Library)

Alarm whistles sounded and were heard by the watchman at 11:30 p.m. The surfboat was launched and quickly evacuated the crew of twelve in less than forty-five minutes. By midnight, the tug, *Ralph*, was on the scene and after pushing the 162-foot *Monohansett* toward shore, directed two streams of water at the conflagration. All night the lifesaving crew worked to salvage as much as possible but the fire was persistent (now fueled by the cargo of coal) and the 34-year-old boat finally succumbed and slid to the bottom. Today, the *Monohansett* is marked by a buoy and can be seen in the clear, shallow waters at the south end of Thunder Bay Island. With no more than a mask and snorkel, one can survey her remains: the charred hull, a large propeller, gearbox, and boiler.

August 26, 1912 - Julia Larsen

The *Julia Larsen* was a 56-ton Canadian schooner bound from Spanish River in the Georgian Bay to Sarnia with a load of lumber. She was 26-years-old and had just been purchased by two brothers-in-law who were making their first trip. Captain Thomas Swanson's wife and their two sons James (4) and George (7) were also on board. Early in the day, they encountered a northwest gale and the two men began pumping furiously to keep her afloat. From Persons' account:

The two men had to pump and make all the effort they could to keep her from water logging. Water kept on gaining so that the schooner became un-manageable and, at 9:45 p.m., she stranded on the ledges of rock on the southeast end of this island.

By this time her sails were also blown away. The No. 2 surfman discovered the wreck and the Beebe-McLellan surf-boat was dispatched, reaching the wreck in about thirty minutes.

According to a newspaper account:

Mrs. Swanson and her children had been sent to the cabin early in the day and the fact that the vessel was close on the island and liable to strike at any time was kept from them. The woman and the children were lying on a cot in the cabin when the shock came. A great torrent of water poured in through a hole in the vessel's side and before she had recovered from the first shock, Mrs. Swanson was separated from her children who were washed about in the little cabin, their cries of terror mingling with those of the mother. After frantic efforts she was able to reach the children again and with her arms about them, crouched in one corner of the cabin prepared for almost anything. The water was up almost to the necks of the children who continued to scream in fright.

The captain and his brother-in-law, James Lawrence, went below and helped Mrs. Swanson and the boys to the deck. Meanwhile, the lifesaving crew attempted to land the surfboat as the sounds of the distressed mother and children mixed with the sounds of the torrential storm. Captain Persons' account continues:

...with jagged rock sticking up all around us, night very dark and a heavy surf....the woman and two children were up on deck where the breakers were sweeping across and they had to cling to the stanchions for their lives. A woman and children could not last under those conditions a great while. The night was so dark the

Julia Larsen. (Photo courtesy of Labadie Collection - Thunder Bay Sanctuary Research Collection, Alpena County Library)

men did not see us until we were right along side and they were frantic in their efforts to signal us, as the lumber was washing off the decks and her spars were likely to fall at any time.

The rocky ledge along the southeast end of Thunder Bay Island created dangerous conditions for the surfboat. As the newspaper account describes:

When the sea is up, the water breaks over the rocks in a manner most baffling to any person trying to approach the shore in a small boat... The slightest false move might have meant the destruction of the lifeboat and great danger to the lives of the men....Under the cool guidance of Captain Persons, the lifesavers managed to reach the Larsen in safety.

Once the family was evacuated from the stranded schooner, the next challenge was to maneuver the surfboat back to the station. Captain Persons described the scene:

The woman fell down her whole length on the bottom of the surf boat, so frightened nothing would induce her to get up. The keeper had to stand straddle of her to handle his boat. Our great danger was in getting on to the rocks where water would not float the surf boat and which would throw us around broad side and capsize us. The keeper kept his boat head to the surf while coming out and trusted the current to sweep him past the shoal...

Captain Persons escorted a weary and pitiful family to the station that night. The loss of the schooner left them destitute, and they were furnished clothing from the Women's National Relief Association stores and provided transportation home on the D. & C. steamer line.

Reminiscing in a 1929 Detroit *News* article, Persons recalled:

When we got within hailing distance, we could hear the children crying. They knew the boat was about to sink and crouched under the bulwarks, drenched with icy water. Their mother was nearly insane from fear. It was the most pitiful sound I ever heard in my life, the crying of those children, and my men worked like devils to get up to the boat. It was risky, very risky indeed. The schooner was so placed among the rocks that it seemed impossible to come along side. One bump and our boat would have been smashed like an eggshell. Just as we took off the last of the passengers, a big wave hit us. It lifted our boat like a feather and swept us between two of the biggest rocks, which we only missed by inches. Yes sir, it was a miracle.

<u>March 21 to 27, 1914 – Fannie A</u>

The *Fannie A.* was a gas fishing boat owned by George Whitten. It had a crew of four plus the Thunder Bay Island lightkeepers on board when it departed Alpena one early March morning. The keepers were being transported to the island to open the lighthouse for the season. Whitten planned to drop them off and then set some nets.

They reached the island around 8:00 a.m. and dropped off the keepers. Whitten then went about setting nets until about noon. On the return home, the *Fannie A.* was caught between two large fields of ice. In a news article he explained:

We came to a standstill with ice piled to a height of 15 feet on either side of the boat... There was no way to get the tug out. She was unharmed but we did not know how soon she would be crushed as an eggshell... My crew consisted of Frank Hoppe, John Cameron and Frank Morey.

According to the wreck report:

Her crew, being afraid she would be crushed, abandoned her about 4:00 p.m. in a little cockle-shell of a boat.

Sugar Island was about a mile away. Whitten explained:

We covered two-thirds of the distance to shore in quick time, walking over solid ice and pulling our rowboat with us. Suddenly the solid ice gave way to thin, newly formed ice and we went splash into the water, saving ourselves by crawling out on the ice and into the boat. Then began our struggle that lasted five hours before we reached the shore. One hundred yards an hour is slow travelling, but it took work to make any progress. We broke the ice with a pike pole and fought on with grim determination.

The lighthouse keeper had been watching the helpless crew and around 5:30 p.m. informed Persons that:

the ice was shoving and he did not think they would ever reach the shore. It was a miracle that their little boat was not cut through by the ice or swept out in the lake.

Meanwhile the weather was deteriorating rapidly. A news article of the day described the scene:

Afloat in a small, frail row boat, in grave danger of having the little craft pierced by sharp, blue ice, Capt. George Whitten and his crew... battled for five hours for their lives in darkness, a blinding snowstorm and biting blizzard that raged Saturday night on Thunder Bay. Drenched to the skin and exhausted, with almost super-human effort the little band of Alpenaites fought bravely on until they reached Sugar Island. Cold and hungry, they searched the dreary, uninhab-

ited island for shelter, finally locating an abandoned shanty. There they built a fire and dried their soaked and frozen garments and longed for daylight, expecting another tough experience to reach Thunder Bay Island where food and warmth awaited them at the lighthouse.

By this time, Captain Persons had contacted the captain of the tug, *Duchess,* and told him about the situation. *"I said I would give him $100 to save those men and their boat."* The *Duchess* steamed out of the harbor at around 7:00 p.m., but four miles out encountered ice and a snow storm and had to turn back. Meanwhile, Persons had assembled his own crew, but with the snow and ice, they decided to wait for daylight. Word had now reached Alpena:

Grave fear was felt that the crew of the Fannie A would ever be seen alive. Anxious watchers expected to be informed of a tragedy.

However, a little after midnight, lighthouse Keeper William Bennett phoned with a message:

A fire had been sighted on Sugar Island and the presumption was that the men were safely landed.

By the next morning, the ice had shifted and strengthened and the crew of the *Fannie A*. was able to simply walk over to Thunder Bay Island. The *Duchess* came out to pick up the crew and returned them to Alpena around noon where they were welcomed and congratulated on their "*narrow escape from death*."

Over the next six days the *Fannie A*. drifted about, carried by the ice floes, and numerous unsuccessful attempts were made to reach her. A friendly rivalry for the $100 reward developed between Capt. H. Ferguson of the *Duchess* and Capt. Fred Couture of the *Isabelle*, but both were forced back by the danger of the "blue ice." On March 24, the *Fannie A.* was eight miles south of Thunder Bay Island, but by March 25, she had drifted northward and was only a mile from the Lincoln fishery on North Point. Two days later, the *Fannie A.* was finally recovered by the *Dutchess*. By this time, she was off Black River Island.

The *Fannie A.* was no stranger to mishap. The lifesavers had previously rescued her three times in one month in 1907 and once again in 1912 due to a disabled engine. And in 1913:

The tug broke from her moorings in the river and was blown into the lake where it was at the mercy of the elements for six days.

<u>May 3, 1929 – O.E. Parks</u>

"Weather Forecast: Wire down. No forecast today."

This terse statement on the front page of the Alpena *News* summed up the conditions that led to the demise of the *O.E. Parks*. Other headlines would have seemed more fitting for a November gale:

O.E. Parks. (Photo courtesy of Labadie Collection - Thunder Bay Sanctuary Research Collection, Alpena County Library)

"Whole Region Hit By Worst May Storm"

"Death Toll May Reach 100 Mark"

The storm brought with it a combination of rain, snow and wind *"of unusual type and duration."*[13] With a crew of nine, the 134-foot steamer was transporting a cargo of pulp wood to Alpena from its home port of Sault Ste. Marie, Canada. The cargo, 225 cords valued at $8000, had been purchased by the Fletcher Paper Company. Departing the Soo on Monday, the steamer first encountered heavy seas as it neared the end of its journey. Around 1:00 a.m. "*The boat passed Middle Island and when about 4 miles east of Thunder Bay Island water began to enter the hold through a broken seam."*

Captain Shields ordered the pumps to be put in operation.

Shields' long experience as a seaman prevented him from becoming unduly alarmed over the situation until he discovered that bark washing off the pulp log cargo had clogged the screens of the pump. Anchors from bow and stern were

Mast of O.E. Parks wreck with lantern hung to warn boat traffic of underwater hazard. (Photo courtesy of Ted Richardson Collection, Michigan Maritime Museum)

[13] Falling barometer readings taken at Thunder Bay Island heralded the storm's approach. At 8:00 a.m. on the 2nd, the barometer read 29.15 and the wind had freshened to a northeast, force 4. 24 hours later the barometer bottomed out at 28.50 and wind was from the northwest in excess of force 7 as the low pressure moved eastward out of the Great Lakes.

dropped. Blazing torches were placed aloft on the rapidly listing vessel and the whistle on the Parks was sounded.

Meanwhile, on Thunder Bay Island, surfman Elmar Olsen was on patrol when, at 2:45 a.m., he heard the distress signal. He reported back to the Coast Guard station. According to Coast Guard Captain E.G. Richardson:

When asked what the weather was like, his reply was that it was hell out, and the expression was well placed. I ordered the crew to get into their heavy weather clothes and man the power lifeboat. Everything in shape, we left the boathouse at 3:30 a.m. It was snowing and blowing so hard that the compass was the only thing I could see. Kept on our compass course until we could pick up the fog signal on the outside of the island. Then took my compass course to where the distress signals were last heard. After rounding the island, it was a battle for the lifeboat to make headway...but the faithful old motor kept pounding away and we picked up the reflection of the flares, which were being sent up by the boat in distress.

The *Parks* was now 3 miles east/northeast of the lighthouse. Captain Shields had persuaded his crew not to abandon ship until help arrived. He warned:

You can't last more than a half-hour in the Parks' lifeboat in such a storm with snow falling rapidly and waves soaring over ten-feet in height. I'll trust my life to the pulp logs rather than take the chance of being capsized.

His crew did not share the captain's optimism and were ready to leave the ship when the sound of the approaching power lifeboat was finally heard. Coast Guard Captain Richardson concluded his narrative:

The first time I came in close, we were showered with clothes and suitcases. I saw something coming at my head and ducked. Surfman Rouleau caught it and got quite a surprise...it was the skipper's dog!

With the rescue of the crew, the work was still not over as the *Parks* had become a hazard to navigation. A note from the lifesaver's logbook a few days later states:

Proceeded to submerged wreck of O.E. Parks 2 miles ENE of Thunder Bay Light and placed light on forward mast as the wreck now lays directly on upper lakes course.

These are just a few, selected shipwreck stories. There are hundreds more to tell and each one has a connection to the Lifesaving and Coast Guard crews who stood watch at Thunder Bay Island. By the time of the *O.E. Parks* incident, a new era had begun in which power lifeboats replaced oar-driven surfboats, radio beacons supplemented the fog whistle and wireless "Mayday" calls replaced distress flags. This, the Coast Guard era, would culminate and bring to a close, 150 years of continuous human presence at Thunder Bay Island.

CHAPTER VII – COAST GUARD

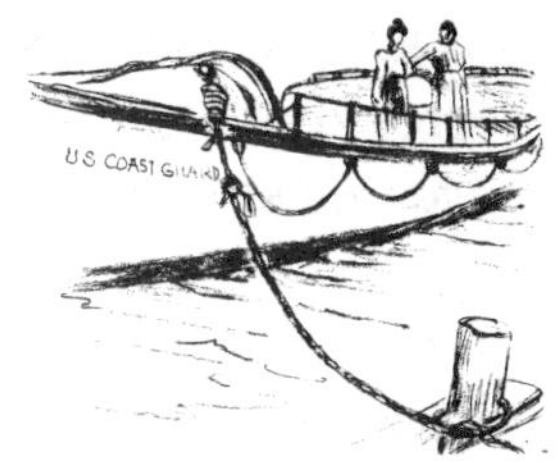

As John Persons went into retirement, a new era began as the Life Saving Service was transformed into the Coast Guard. On a practical level, this resulted in few changes at the island. The lighthouse was still operated independently by the Lighthouse Service. In 1915, John H. Oles took over as captain of the station, and then in 1916 he was replaced by Robert Hodge. In 1917 the station was assigned an identifying number, "252." Gone were the dramatic rescue narratives. A review of the 225 "Assistance Record" forms from 1917 through 1935 shows the routine duties of the crew:

Transporting between the island and North Point	31%
Towing vessels to harbor	17%

Coast Guard crew in front of old Lifesaving Station in 1916 - the year after the Lifesaving Service became part of the Coast Guard. (Photo courtesy of Central Michigan University - Clarke Historical Library)

Assisting vessels with engine trouble	16%
Searching for missing vessels	12%
Rescuing stranded vessels	9%

Other duties included:
*warning vessels away from shore using Coston flare signals
*transporting fuel tanks and re-lighting gas buoys
*towing drifting pound net stakes
*transporting Weather Bureau, Lighthouse Service and bird banding crews

Besides observations of weather and sea conditions, the daily log kept by the Captain included the list of watches, beach patrols and vessels sighted[14]. The following is Robert Hodge's narrative from a typical day – September 20, 1917:

At 7 a.m. tested telephone, line working well. Performing morning duties, turned engine of powerboat. At 8 a.m. morning colors, all members stood at attention and saluted, inspected station buildings, grounds and apparatus; Result satisfactory. Crew employed from 8:30 a.m. to 11:30 a.m. wheeling wood from the dock. Practiced with wigwag and semaphore signals from 1 to 2 p.m. At 2 p.m. launched surf-boat No.444 and drilled under oars for 1 hour. Drilled with beach apparatus from 3:10 to 3:40 p.m. Time: 3 minutes 45 seconds, aim good, elevation 12 degrees, moderate breeze north, used No. 7 braided shot line and 1-1/2 ounces of powder. Sand anchor 75 yards from wreck pole. At 4 p.m. changed dials, lookout and patrol duty properly performed. Evening colors at 5:50 p.m., all members stood at attention and saluted. At 8 p.m. made careful inspection of all station buildings and boats. At 11 p.m. repeated inspection. Results satisfactory.

[14] At the turn of the century, it was not uncommon to sight as many as 25 schooners and 65 steamers in a single day.

Motorized lifeboat (right) and ice skiff (left) circa 1920's. The ice skiff was pulled by hand over the ice to open water. (Photo courtesy of Ted Richardson Collection, Michigan Maritime Museum)

While the station was typically closed from late December until March, the Captain and one other crewman stayed on for the winter and continued to perform routine maintenance, tests of the telephone and weather observations.

In 1930, a new Coast Guard Station was built. Construction began in early August for a two-story structure. In early December, the building was complete. According to the Alpena *News:*

Every modern facility and convenience is embodied in the new building constructed at the island... at a cost of $15,000. Running water, showers, baths, and electric lights are among the up-to-date conveniences available.

The family of the Coast Guard Officer-In-Charge would often come out to spend time on the island during the summer. They would stay in the original 1876 station, which had been left standing but rarely used since the new station was opened. In the 1930's, the lighthouse keepers' families were also on the island and the children became playmates for the summer.

Newly Constructed Coast Guard Station - 1930. Note the "wreck pole" at left used as a target when performing breeches buoy drills. (Photo courtesy of U.S. Coast Guard Historian)

Kay Richardson shared memories from her husband, Ted, whose father was in charge at the island during the 1920's and 1930's:

The kids quickly fell into the free reign of summer fun. There was berry-picking, fishing and swimming to enjoy. The girls loved to pick wildflowers – lady slippers, jack-in-the-pulpit and trillium.

The young surfmen stationed delighted in having Ted go on the three-mile beach patrol each sundown with them or to stand lookout in the high tower.

Some summer evenings were spent with the lighthouse people, enjoying a potluck supper and having a huge beach bonfire for roasting marshmallows. Seeing the boat traffic after dark was memorable, especially the great D & C passenger boats heading for Mackinac Island with their lights glistening.

Phyllis Richardson Everly, Ted's sister, first visited the island when she was eight years old and recalls that a motor surf-boat would make a daily trip to North Point to transport personnel. Once a month the lifeboat was taken to Alpena for supplies. "*There were lots of snakes on the island,*" she recalled, "*and the children treated them like pets and fed them spiders.*" Phyllis has fond memories of swimming in the lake. "*There were lots of snakes there too, and Dad wouldn't let us go in the water until it was 68 degrees. We also enjoyed playing baseball, square dancing and collecting berries for jam with the lighthouse keeper's children. One time we visited*

Captain E.G. Richardson at Thunder Bay Island in 1937. Note old breeches buoy "Manby" mortar below signal bell. (Photo courtesy of Ted Richardson Collection, Michigan Maritime Museum)

the lighthouse keepers at Middle Island and after a potluck supper, sat on the beach that warm summer evening watching the Port Huron to Mackinac race boats sail by."

But Phyllis' favorite memory was waking up early one morning and walking the path with her father to the watchtower where they witnessed a glorious sunrise over Lake Huron.

Similarly, Bill Adrian whose father was officer in the 1940's recalled these memories:

We had many great days on the island with dad and the sailors. When we were not fishing, exploring, chasing snakes or just having fun, we were polishing doorknobs, mowing grass, painting or walking patrol with the duty man.

The annual sailboat race, Port Huron to Mackinac, would invariably see boats cutting between the island and the mainland, only to be grounded on the huge rocks. We would rescue the men and tow the boats into Alpena harbor. The road to the docks at North Point by Woelks' cottage had to be maintained also. Food supplies from the Marine Market and Krueger's Market were run back on this road. In the evenings, we had no radio and it was long before TV so we learned to play cribbage, pinochle and even poker with chips for money.

The men kept a live fish box in the boat house, filled with perch and green bass, so fresh fish was always on hand.

In 1937, the Coast Guard Stations at both Middle Island and Sturgeon Point were closed and Alcona *Herald* writer R.E. Prescott commented:

Development of power lifeboats, motorized shore equipment and radio communications, permitting the coverage of wide area in minimum time allowed one station to do the work of two or three as compared with oar-powered days.

That one station would be, for the time, Thunder Bay Island.

The following recollections of former Thunder Bay Island Coastguardsmen Paul Rehkopf, Jim Messer, Ralph Gates, Jack LaForest and Walt Plohocky give an impression of daily life during the 1950's, 1960's and 1970's.

Paul Rehkopf was stationed at Thunder Bay Island in 1955. During that year the old attached lighthouse keeper's quarters were remodeled so the crew was crowded into the old 2nd Assistant Keeper's quarters. Such confinement led to tensions that year. "*Thunder Bay Island was not a desirable posting. You were assigned there – you did not volunteer.*" During that year the island's electrical systems were upgraded from DC to AC and new diesel generators replaced the old gasoline-driven ones. Paul recalls that the fog signal was powered by compressed air from two Ingersoll-Rand compressors. These were started with a gas "pony" engine and then switched over to oil. The temperature of the engine was regulated by rolling a canvas curtain up or down. One time the fog signal ran for 28 days continuously. *"When it was finally turned off one night, I bolted up in bed, startled by the sudden silence."*

Paul recalls that on a clear night the Sturgeon Point light could be seen – over twenty-five miles away. And he remembers having to keep the three Seth Thomas clocks used for the radio beacon to within three seconds of the Bureau of Standards time signal.

James Messer was second generation Coast Guard. Born in Tawas in 1929, he started boot camp in 1949 at Cape May,

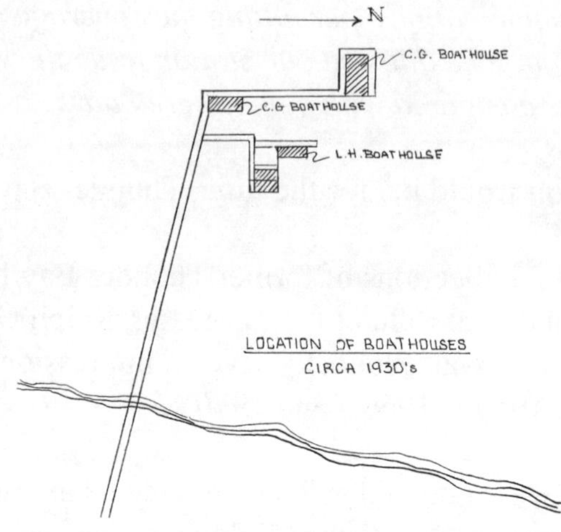

Boat docks circa 1940. (Photo courtesy of Paula Glennie)

New Jersey. Over the years, he served at a variety of remote postings: Cape Cod Lightship, Charlevoix Crib Light (Lansing Shoals), Poverty Island, Chambers Island and in Japan. When asked if there was something that attracted him to islands, Messer explained that he enjoyed the quiet and "*being left alone with no one to bother you*." He served at

Thunder Bay Island both in the 1950's and 1960's with his last assignment as Officer in Charge for two seasons before retiring in 1968. The officer and crew lived in the old 1868 lighthouse keeper's quarters. By this time, the Coast Guard buildings on the west-side of the island had been abandoned. He worked three weeks on, one week off and earned $77 per month. About half of that went to groceries.

"*It was just a duty station,*" explained Messer. Those duties included maintaining the lighthouse, fog signal and radio beacon, monitoring radio traffic, taking weather readings and relaying them to the Weather Bureau, displaying weather signal flags and maintaining fuel supplies. While rescues were generally delegated to helicopters from the Traverse City Coast Guard, Messer and the Thunder Bay Island crew were able to assist with two shipwrecks: the *Nordmeer* and the *Royalton*.

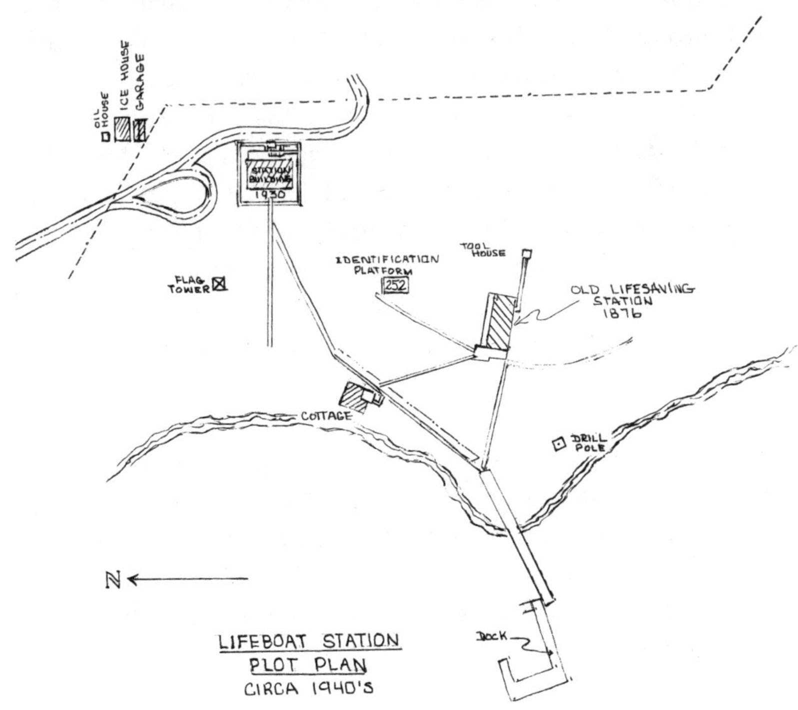

LIFEBOAT STATION PLOT PLAN
CIRCA 1940'S

Pastimes included beachcombing, rabbit and goose hunting, and bird banding. "*We didn't do much hook-and-line fishing, but on occasion we'd go out with a couple of buckets and lift a few gill nets for some fresh fish.*" Messer had a beagle and would take him over to Sugar Island from time-to-time. The beagle would swim back to Thunder Bay Island following the boat. During the years he was stationed at Thunder Bay Island, the water levels were very low and they could not use the 25-foot launch assigned to the station. Instead, they resorted to an 18-foot air-cooled motorized ice skiff with runners.

Ralph Gates served at Thunder Bay Island from 1963 until his retirement in 1965. He remembers that "*although it was a seven man station, they were always short with only four or five at a time.*" The greatest challenge was monitoring the fog signal and radio beacon and keeping them coordinated. Gates recalls that they were generally stationed at the island from April through December. At the end of the season, the *Acacia* would take them off the island. He also remembers a jeep that was used on the island. Though it only had four or five hundred miles on it, *"it was pretty well beat up.*" Gates did not venture off as much as Messer. He explains that the ubiquitous poison ivy kept him close to the station most of the time. When one of the crew went on leave or needed supplies, they would take the boat to North Point where the Alpena Lighthouse crew would meet them and shuttle them to town.

In April, 1961, the Coast Guard Cutter *Acacia* docked at Thunder Bay Island and off stepped 21-year-old Engineman Jack LaForest to his new posting. He spent two seasons on the island and became fascinated with this unique location and its history. Here is an interview between the author and LaForest which took place in 2003.

What was it like when you first arrived?

The Acacia brought the crew and heavy supplies to the island in the spring and was also the ship that picked up the crew at the end of the season in the fall. The first day on the island was spent hauling supplies, repairing frozen pipes from the winter, and re-stringing the radio beacon antenna, which had come down over the winter. Gasoline for the Jeep and boat motor was transported in 55 gallon drums which were pushed off a barge, lines tied to them and hauled ashore with the Jeep. The barge also carried fuel oil, which was pumped through a pipeline from the dock to a 10,000 gallon fuel storage tank which stood next to the fog signal building.

Twenty-five foot work boat - 1950's. (Photo courtesy of Paula Glennie)

What was the routine at Thunder Bay Island?

We would stand watches (four hours on, eight hours off) and then work regular hours from 8:00 a.m. until 4:00 p.m. The crew was kept busy scraping and painting buildings and boats, servicing equipment and keeping the station clean. I would give a lot of credit to Jim Messer who served as Officer-In-Charge for keeping the station "ship shape." We also operated a station for the Weather Bureau and would provide reports every six hours by phone. Every year we would assist the DNR in bird banding of gulls, great blue herons and night herons. During my two seasons, I banded over 7000 birds. Since we were on "isolated duty," we would work 28 days on and then have seven days off. You were always praying for good weather when it was your turn to depart for the seven days of compensatory leave.

<u>How would you break up the monotony of your daily duties on the island?</u>

Visits from civilians were always a treat. When people asked if it was OK to tie up to the dock, we would facetiously request a case of beer for the privilege. Some stayed overnight at the dock and we got to know them. Some were simply taking shelter from the weather on trips up or down the lake. Sometimes we got to be involved with them in a stressful situation where we could aid and comfort them and be privy to their strengths and their weaknesses. We thought we had died and gone to heaven when we learned that the captain of a sailboat we towed off a reef in Misery Bay was a large downstate beer distributor. He was very appreciative and came back on occasion to bring us some "cheer." There were SCUBA divers like Jack Thompson, Bill Bunting, Sunny Baker, Dick Weinkauf, Rick Piper and Dick Hunter. I became interested in the sport while I was at Thunder Bay Island.

We also spent our free time on walks along the shore or in the woods, fishing at the boathouse, watching storm waves come ashore, and hunting. There was always one man on watch and one man on leave, and sometimes we were a man short so you had to entertain yourself. Sometimes we would take the skiff to Sugar or Gull Island to spear carp during spawning season. Anything that landed on the island was considered fair game by some of the crewmen. The year before I arrived, so the story goes, a flight of Canadian geese fighting a headwind and needing rest landed on the north end

Left to Right: Weather Bureau Storm Signal Tower, Old lookout and New lookout tower - 1940. (Photo courtesy of Paula Glennie)

of the island. Some of the crew took their guns and began pursuing them from island to island. When all was said and done, only two escaped and the rest were enough to fill two refrigerators.

<u>What facilities were on the island at the time?</u>

There were the station building, garage, light tower, fog signal and boathouse. The fog signal building consisted of a watch shack, engine room, and radio beacon building. The electronics were inside a soundproof watch room and the engine room housed two diesel generators, which provided electricity and powered the two 3-stage air compressors for the fog horn. The generators were alternated and operated 24/7. There was a 25-foot work boat with a 4-cylinder Gray Marine diesel that could do six knots with a following sea. It had a heavy oak skeg six-inches wide, eighteen-inches deep and filled with lead. If I had my druthers in a storm, that's the boat I would ask for. We also had a 14-foot skiff with a 10 horsepower outboard. I also had my own 22-foot Chris Craft Sedan. There was also the old lifesaving station, which burned to the ground in 1962[15]*.*

What were the living quarters like?

They were good. The Officer in Charge had his private room and the rest of us bunked two to a room according to rank. There was a large living room on the south side of the house and a galley on the north. The Officer in Charge's office was between the galley and the passageway to the light tower. We had an electric washing machine, dryer, refrigerator, freezer, cooking range, water heater, furnace and automatic chlorinator for drinking water. Our water supply was from the lake and pumped every other week with a portable pump up to a wooden storage tank in the garage. Cooking and cleaning chores were rotated on a weekly basis. We each received $90.00 per month. Each person returning from leave would do grocery shopping.

What methods of communication were available?

We had a battery powered crank phone system, which connected the facilities on the island via cable to the mainland at North Point. There was also a 25-watt marine radio in the watch shack. If all else fails, we could signal one another by firing up the foghorn and giving it a few blasts. Inside the watch shack was the radio beacon, which transmitted the Morse code letter "K" at ten minutes before and twenty minutes past the hour. Three grandfather style clocks timed it to the second.

[15] According to the Coast Guard historian, the buildings had been abandoned in 1951. The Coast Guard had tried to sell the old buildings with no success. Jack took "home movies" of both the 1876 and 1930 buildings being set on fire. The same movie shows a crew erecting a radio tower designed to improve the station's radio link with Alpena.

Were you involved in any rescues?

We were too under-manned to be a Search and Rescue station and our 25-foot boat was too slow. Most situations we handed off to the Coast Guard auxiliary with their faster boats or called Traverse City Airbase or Tawas. Jim Messer was very cautious about sending the boat out in rough weather which meant that we were often weathered-in either going or coming back from leave.

Fishing has always been a popular pastime at Thunder Bay Island, beginning with the first lighthouse keeper in 1831. Here are Coast Guardsmen from the 1950's with their catch of Lake Trout. (Photo courtesy of Paula Glennie)

What other memories do you have of your experience on the island?

It may sound crazy, but while we were there it was quite common knowledge that there was some "spirit" or "ghost" that one would encounter when walking at night between our station and the fog signal building. One fellow was so scared that he insisted on driving the jeep to and from the fog signal building. Something spooks me about Sugar Island as well. One time I was camping there during a terrible storm and I heard footsteps outside my tent. I had my pistol and I fired two warning shots. There was no sign of anyone."[16]

In May 1969, the Alpena *News* did a profile of the Coast Guardsmen serving at Thunder Bay Island. At the time there were five men at the station. "Watch" duties consisted mostly of monitoring marine radio transmissions. The men worked three-week stints followed by a week's leave. At the season's end in December, they were given 51 days leave. The article mentions that search-and-rescue was not typically performed; however, *"six such calls were answered last year."*

The following year Walt Plohocky was transferred from his position as keeper of the Alpena Light to Thunder Bay Island. At the beginning of the season, the crew was transported to the island in a helicopter and spent the first few days getting the buildings and equipment back in shape. During Walt's tenure, the station became more involved in search and rescue missions with the use of a 25-foot "double-ender" motor surf-boat. North Point was not used as much and most "logistics runs" were made directly to Alpena harbor.

Walt recalled that there were the remains of an old rifle range at the north end of the island that had been used by various Coast Guard stations over the years for training. The fog signal was operated whenever North Point (about five miles away) was no longer visible. The foghorn was so loud that when the crew needed to display weather flags, they would drive the jeep to the tower and wait for the few seconds that the horn was silent, before dashing out to hoist the flags.

At the end of the season, the boats were hoisted into the boat-house, the water lines drained, and the electrical system shut

[16] According to Frederick Stonehouse, Ted Richardson reported that during the 1930's and 1940's the lighthouse at Thunder Bay Island was haunted by the ghost of a former keeper named "Morgan." Coast Guardsmen of later years also reported a phantom keeper that would appear on the tower and a ghostly family that appeared, dressed as pioneers, in the trees along the path to the fog signal building.

down. Then the crew prayed for good weather so the helicopter could get them off the island and home in time for Christmas. During Walt's career, he had assignments at a variety of lighthouses around the country, but Thunder Bay Island remained his favorite. He particularly liked being around the fresh water, roaming the open spaces, and "*being your own boss.*"

As time went by, radar, LORAN and helicopters diminished the importance of the Thunder Bay Island station. In November 1980, the station was formally closed, the light automated and the island abandoned.

An era has ended with the closure earlier this month of Light Station Thunder Bay, the second to last manned offshore light station in the Great Lakes...Thunder Bay Island is deserted and machines run the beacons instead of man.

Alpena *News*

The island was now abandoned to the elements, and only the occasional campers, scuba divers and Coast Guard maintenance crews would come to visit. Over fifteen years would pass before interest in preserving this special place would motivate a group of citizens to become its caretakers.

"Liberty Boat" used by Coast Guard in the 1940's. Captain Ray Anderson. (Photo courtesy of Paula Glennie)

Partial List of Coast Guard Officers in Charge at Thunder Bay Island

John H. Oles	1915 – 1916
Robert Hodges	1916 – 1919
David M. Small	1919 – 1923
A.R. Davidson	1924 – 1926
E.G. Richardson	1927 – 1929
J.G. Liedke	1930 – 1932
H.A. Peterson	1933 –
E.G. Richardson	1934 – 1937
Alexander Rouleau	1938 –
John F. Glaza	1938 – 1939
Ray Anderson	1940 –
Arthur H.W. Adrian	1946 – 1949
Charles Poirier	1952 –
Gustav Hans Zier	1953 – 1954
Charles LaFaver	1955 –
James Messer	1961 – 1962
Ed Pryczinski	1962 – 1963
Ralph Gates	1963 – 1965
James Messer	1966 – 1968
Jarvis L. Roark	1969 –
Walt Plohocky	1970 – 1974

CHAPTER VIII - PRESERVATION

The end of the Coast Guard era on Thunder Bay Island began in 1980. This was the year the light was automated and the crew reassigned. In 1984, the lighthouse was placed on the National Register of Historic Places. However, over the next decade, the only constant at Thunder Bay Island was the gradual deterioration of the remaining structures (the lighthouse, lighthouse keeper's quarters, oil house, fog signal building, dock and boat house).

In 1990, an environmental study of the island was commissioned by the Coast Guard. The purpose was "*to identify the potential existence of environmental contamination associated with nine dump sites identified on the island.*" Historical data was studied to locate sites and surface soil samples were taken for analysis. The nine sites included a generator house ("Grassis Shack"), heliport, and five dumps scattered about the island. The report provided detailed chemical analysis of soil samples.

This was followed in August 1993 by a general cleanup of the island, removing 175 cubic yards of trash and hazardous waste using helicopter transported dumpsters. The Coast Guard Cutter *Acacia* landed a crew of twenty for the effort. This was the first such project in the Coast Guard's 9th District, and an official was quoted in the Alpena *News* that "*Thunder Bay Island was picked as the premier project because it was probably the worst site we had in the district.*"

Then in 1995, the Coast Guard decided to "excess and grantout" the property through the Bureau of Land

Management (BLM). The first party to look over the property was the U.S. Fish and Wildlife Service. This prompted a group of local citizens to become concerned about both the accessibility and preservation of the lighthouse. They were concerned that the Fish and Wildlife Service might not adequately protect the cultural resources and human history of the island.

Dick Moehl, president of the Great Lakes Lighthouse Keepers Association, was contacted to provide advice on how the lighthouse could be preserved. Mr. Moehl met with a group of concerned citizens, the "Future Keepers of the Thunder Bay Island Light Station," at a meeting in January 1996. The purpose of the meeting was fourfold:

*Determine the level of local interest in accepting responsibility for the landmark.

*Outline the steps to be taken in forming a non-profit organization and establishing a Board of Directors and Working Committee structure.

Drummond Islander II runs into shoaling off Thunder Bay Island

The tug Drummond Islander II, with a barge carrying a large crane en route to Au Gres, struck shoaling just off Thunder Bay Island Thursday morning. There was significant damage to the hull of the vessel as it hit rocks in shallow water and opened the bottom of the boat. The tug and barge was pushed to shallow water where temporary repairs were done through the day. The Drummond Islander II was brought into Lafarge late Thursday night where it will receive further repairs. There were four people on board and no reported injuries. A representative of the Coast Guard said he wasn't sure of monetary damage, but believes it will be significant given there were 4-foot gashes in the hull.

October 2003

Even with recent advances in navigational aids, sailors still come to grief at Thunder Bay Island. (Photo courtesy of David Wobser)

*Develop a fundraising plan.

*Begin the process of obtaining a lease through the Coast Guard and Bureau of Land Management.

In less than two years, the Thunder Bay Island Preservation Society (TBIPS) had been established and over 60 members recruited. $3000 had been raised and over 400 volunteer hours had been spent working on the island. In addition, permission had been received from the Coast Guard, Bureau of Land Management and State Historian to begin preservation efforts. These accomplishments were communicated to Senator Levin in a letter from Gerald Broad (president of the TBIPS) in September of 1997. In the same letter, Mr. Broad outlined concerns about the Fish and Wildlife Service

Interior of Fog Signal Building in 2003. (Photo courtesy of Dave Wobser)

possibly thwarting preservation efforts if it obtained sole possession of the island. At the time, most of the island was being managed by the Fish and Wildlife Service. As Mr. Broad exhorted on behalf of the society:

Nature and man have co-existed on Thunder Bay Island since 1832, and we see no reason that this should not continue. We believe that the public should have access to this area so they can appreciate the historical significance of the Light Station and, at the same time, be able to view the wonderful natural features of forest and wildlife on the island. The members of our organization are dedicated to doing everything possible to preserve and restore Thunder Bay Island Light Station if we only can get access to it.

Mr. Broad then requested Senator Levin's assistance in obtaining a "Legislative Transfer." Previous efforts had been made through U.S. Representative Bart Stupak who challenged TBIPS and the Fish and Wildlife Service to "come to some sort of agreement."

On December 1, 1997 a ten-year lease was signed between the Coast Guard and TBIPS for Thunder Bay Island *"containing only those portions necessary to access, maintain, restore and preserve the following improvements…."* The improvements listed included the light tower, attached dwelling, fog signal building, paint locker (old oilhouse),

Restoration work at fog signal building. (Photo courtesy of Thunder Bay Island Preservation Society)

boathouse, concrete walkways and tramway.

The lease allowed for use of the buildings *"in a historic setting (museum)"* and required that all work be done in compliance with the Advisory Council on Historic Preservation and the State Historical Preservation Officer.

As this book goes to press, the TBIPS has developed a partnership with Alpena Township and is creating the management plan necessary to pursue an administrative transfer of the historically significant portions of the island. Work has also commenced on restoration of the cracked lighthouse tower and is being funded by a Michigan Department of Environmental Quality grant.

Those who visit the island today are captivated by its remarkable features – the historic lighthouse, the rare wildflowers, the many shipwrecks which litter the surrounding waters, the underwater cliffs, the historic rock carvings and, most of all, the serenity and rugged beauty. It truly is, "magnificent in its desolation" and deserves the utmost care and preservation for future generations.

"Magnificent Desolation" - Thunder Bay Island in 1886. (Photo courtesy of Jesse Besser Museum)

Milestones – Thunder Bay Island Preservation Society

Jan - 1996 TBIPS incorporates and requests long term historic lease of lighthouse from Coast Guard.

Jun - 1996 Coast Guard and TBIPS tour island. Five-year plan submitted to Coast Guard Lt. Commander in Cleveland

Oct - 1996 First Annual Great Lakes Lighthouse Festival in Alpena. Permission granted by BLM and Michigan State Historical Preservation Office to TBIPS to make improvements at island.

May - 1997 TBIPS obtains "vote of confidence" from County and Township in effort to obtain title to Light Station.

Aug – 1997 In Alpena *News* article, Fish and Wildlife Service states intentions to obtain lighthouse from BLM.

Dec – 1997 TBIPS obtains lease from Coast Guard.

Mar - 2001 Michigan Department of Environmental Quality "Clean Water Initiative Redevelopment Grant" offered to TBIPS/Alpena Township lighthouse for restoration of tower.

May – 2003 Meeting held between TBIPS, Fish and Wildlife Service, Bureau of Land Management and Alpena Township to discuss method for transfer of portions of island to TBIPS.

Jan – 2004 U.P. Engineers completes a condition assessment report for the lighthouse tower to define the scope of repairs. The project is to be bid in spring, 2004.

APPENDICES

APPENDIX I - THE LEGENDS

While researching the history of Thunder Bay Island, I often found stories that could not be verified historically, but are nonetheless part of its legend.

JULE CHARDIN – OR THE SMUGGLERS OF THUNDER BAY – This short story was written by Alpena *News* city editor George Waldron and published in July, 1914. According to Waldron, *"This story is founded on facts. The narrative is real, many of the characters actual, but the names, except in one or two instances, are fictitious. The scenes are laid around the Thunder Bay group of islands and on the mainland from 1847 to 1851"*

Synopsis –
The story is told of the Chardin family who resided with other fishermen as squatters on Thunder Bay Island. Jule and Gretchen Chardin had two children – Wilhelmina ("Mina") and Pierre. Pierre sails on the schooner *Petrel* under Capt. Anderson. Jule is a fisherman, but also engaged in illegal smuggling of whiskey, which is brought to the island by the *Petrel* on its uplake trips.

Jule had come to the island in 1845, fleeing from Canada due to his involvement in the MacKenzie Rebellion of 1837. He becomes the informal "leader" figure among the fishermen. By 1847 there was a population of over 170 in the fishing village with 30 fishing sloops which deployed trap and seine nets. There was a rude dock for shallow steamers and schooners where fish, cargo and passengers were loaded. The fishing season lasted from spring to November and though the fishing villagers are considered "squatters," they are not bothered by the government. There was also a schoolteacher and a chapel for visiting preachers.

Jule becomes friends with other "criminal" types including past murderers, burglars, and counterfeiters. This group is under the vigilant eye of government agents who visit the island at various times under disguise.

There were two steamboats that regularly served the island: *Madison* and *Oriole*. In November the last steamer calls on the island. About half the population leaves for the winter. The remaining are isolated until May when the first steamboat arrives. The only contact with the outside world during the long winter is an occasional dogsled run from Devil River with the mail.

In the summer of 1848, an eviction notice is given by the government to the fishermen – pay rent or leave the island. While it generates concern among the squatters, the government does not seem intent on enforcing it immediately. When, in 1848, the *Petrel* catches fire and sinks off the island, Jule decides to get out of the smuggling business for good. But his life is about to take a new and difficult turn.

In the summer of 1849, government land officials, accompanied by a U.S. Marshall, return to the island and give July 15 as the deadline for the squatters to leave. Many fishing families move to North Point and Sugar Island, but thirty, with Chardin as leader, remain. On July 15, fifty soldiers under Capt. Moreland arrive from the Mackinac Garrison. Tensions build and on the fourth day of the standoff, the soldiers fire their guns just over the heads of the squatters. Conceding defeat, the squatters reluctantly leave the island.

STRANGE CURRENTS OF THUNDER BAY ISLAND

According to Fred Landon's book, Lake Huron, *"Records compiled at the Coast Guard station at Thunder Bay... showed that ninety five percent of all the groundings or strandings in that vicinity were the result of vessels being carried off their course by the currents during thick weather."* Landon goes on to claim that there are strange flows around the island that do not correspond with the prevailing northerly currents or the current wind conditions. *"...a few years ago a Coast Guard at Thunder Bay observed an ice floe travelling directly into the teeth of a moderate northwest gale at a pace faster than he could walk."*

Captain Persons related his own tales of what he called the "back sea" in a Detroit *News* article of December 2, 1931:

The back sea swirls around this coast... That's the thing that sets ships topsy turvy and off their course. I learned that in the 38 years I was watching things around that island. I've seen ice floes running straight into the wind. It's terrific, I tell you, that back sea. It crowds and crowds a poor ship shoreward and the skipper don't know what's happening to him until—smack! He's hit a rock or something.

In 1911, Captain Persons was consulted during an inquiry on the Lake Superior wreck of the *Acadia.* During the course of the inquiry, he related what he learned at Thunder Bay Island:

Many captains coming up the lake think they will land outside Thunder Bay Island somewhere, and coming up find themselves inside the island two or three miles. The first remark made with an oath, is "how did I get in here?"

<u>BAYFIELD'S 1822 SURVEY: THE MYSTERY LIGHT-HOUSE</u>

Alpena historian Trelfa had exhibited an excerpt of a map reported to be an original 1822 survey of Thunder Bay by Capt. W.H. Bayfield. Looking closely at the map, a lighthouse is discerned on the southeast corner of the island. This raises the question: Was there a previous lighthouse to the one constructed in 1831? Interest in this matter was further piqued since mention of a "wooden" lighthouse (assumed to be the first) is found in some articles about Thunder Bay Island and a popular book on Michigan ghost towns.

However, this writer obtained a copy of the original 1822 survey from the University of Western Ontario – Geography Department and no lighthouse is shown. However, the same source provided an 1864 chart based on Bayfield's original survey which, in fact, does show the lighthouse. Clearly, this was the chart Trefla had previously found, but incorrectly dated.

APPENDIX II - THUNDER BAY ISLAND CHRONOLOGY

1679 – Thunder Bay Island described by Louis Hennepin during journey with Lasalle on the *Griffin*.

1830 – Appropriation for lighthouse on Thunder Bay Island.

1831 – Construction begun. First tower collapses during storm.

1832 – Construction completed. First lighthouse keeper appointed: Jesse Muncey.

1835 – William Cullings first fisherman.

1842 – Thunder Bay Island designated "government reservation."

1847 – New lighthouse keeper dwelling constructed.

1849 – Wreck of the sidewheel steamer, *New Orleans*, near Sugar Island.

1857 – Lighthouse rebuilt and equipped with Fresnel lens.

1858 – Fog signal bell installed.

1859 – John Paxton purchases Sugar Island and moves fishery operation there.

1860 – First Assistant Light Keeper position established.

1865 – Wreck of *Pewabic*.

1868 – Attached lighthouse keeper's quarters constructed.

1871-1872 – Steam fog whistle building constructed.

1874 – Life Saving Station appropriation approved for Thunder Bay Island.

1875 – Lighthouse constructed at mouth of Thunder Bay River in Alpena.

1876 – Life Saving Station opens under Captain Issac Matthews.

1877 - John Persons appointed Captain of Life Saving Station.

1884 - Stormhouse added to keeper's quarters. Tramway constructed for delivery of coal to fog signal buildings.

1889 – Storm damages light station and destroys tramway.

1891 – Tramway rebuilt.

1892 – New landing dock built for lighthouse.

1894 – A second fog signal was purchased and installed.

1895 – Telephone service installed between Alpena, Thunder Bay Island, Middle Island and North Point. Weather Bureau station established.

1901 – Assistant lighthouse keeper's quarters remodeled.

1903 – Brick oil-house constructed.

1907 – Cement walks installed at lighthouse. Wooden cistern replaced with a brick cistern. Second Assistant Light Keeper position established. Brick fog signal building completed.

1909 – Life Saving Station begins using 34-foot power lifeboat.

1913 – Lamp converted from "oil wick" to "incandescent oil vapor."

1914 – Life Saving Service merged into Coast Guard.

1916 – Old fog signal building moved and remodeled into residence for Second Assistant Light Keeper and family.

1920 – Permission granted to U.S. Navy to occupy areas at Lighthouse complex. Radio Compass Station installed near lighthouse.

1921 – Type C Diaphone fog signal installed.

1926 – Radio Beacon Antenna installed between two towers near fog signal building.

1927 – Radio Station Building erected near fog signal building. Navy occupation of Life Saving Station complex areas cancelled.

1930 – New Coast Guard station built.

1932 – Type F Diaphone fog signal installed. Addition to 2nd Assistant Keeper's dwelling. Addition to fog signal building for fuel storage.

1938 – Cement coating applied over surface of lighthouse.

1939 – Lighthouse Service merged into Coast Guard.

1944 – Feasibility study of relocating Coast Guard station to North Point.

1955 – Attached lighthouse keeper's quarters remodeled.

1962 – Old Coast Guard & Life Saving Stations burned to the ground.

1980 – Lighthouse automated and station closed.

1984 – Lighthouse designated to National Historic Register.

1990 – Environmental study of Thunder Bay Island.

1996 – Archaeology study by Michigan State University students.

1997 – Portions of island transferred to Thunder Bay Island Preservation Society in a ten-year lease.

2000 – Thunder Bay designated a National Marine Sanctuary.

APPENDIX III - DESCRIPTION OF ROCK CARVINGS

There are two sites of rock carvings on the limestone slabs that form the eastern shore of the island. Over 50 carvings exist dating from as early as the 1870's and as recent as the 1990's. Some of the notable names include:

B.H. Persons – brother of Captain John Persons

USLSS Crew of 1879

USLHS Crew from Detroit (1929)

H.D. Ferris – Surfman at Thunder Bay Island and later Coast Guard Captain

W.R. Bennetts – Lighthouse Keeper (1902 – 1919)

F.B. Case – Surfman

Capt. E.G. Richardson – Coast Guard Captain

B.L. Richardson – son of Captain E.G. Richardson

Audrey Richardson – daughter of Captain E.G. Richardson

J.D. Holmes – Civil War veteran, prominent Alpena attorney and husband to Captain John Persons' sister, Minnie D.

W.A. Comstock – Democrat governor of Michigan from Alpena (1933-1934)

Joseph K. Persons – surfman

Celia Persons – wife of Captain John Persons

Ben Teno - surfman

REFERENCES

CHAPTER I – NATURAL HISTORY

Devonian Strata of Alpena and Presque Isle Counties, Michigan by George M. Ehlers, 1970.

"Alvars of Michigan" – Published by the Michigan Natural Features Inventory, Lansing, MI, 1998.

"Great Lakes Bedrock Shores of Michigan" - Published by the Michigan Natural Features Inventory, Lansing, MI, 1997.

Interview with Tyrone Black, C.P.G., Senior Geologist with the Michigan Department of Natural Resources.

"Traverse Rocks of the Thunder Bay Region, Michigan" by Aldred S. Warthin, Jr. and G. Arthur Cooper - Published in the Bulletin of the American Association of Petroleum Geologists. May, 1943.

Michigan Islands National Wildlife Refuge – website: http://midwest.fws.gov/shiawassee/michiganislands.com.

"Biodiversity Investment Areas – Nearshore Terrestrial Ecosystems" by Ron Reid, Karen Rodriquez and Amy Mysz – Published by State of the Lakes Ecosystem Conference. July, 1999.

CHAPTER II – EARLY HISTORY

Atlas of Great Lakes Indian History by Helen Hornbeck Tanner, 1987.

Michigan – A History of the Wolverine State by Willis F. Dunbar & George S. May, 1980.

Michigan – A History by Bruce Catton, 1984.

The Michigan Fur Trade by Ida Amanda Johnson, 1919.

The Fate of the Griffon by Harrison John McLean, 1974.

Schoolcraft's Narrative Journal of Travels edited by Mentor L. Williams, 1992.

Stories the Red People Have Told and More by Robert E. Haltiner, 2002.

"Overview Study of Archaeological and Cultural Values on Shiawassee, Michigan Islands, and Wyandotte National Wildlife Refuges in Saginaw, Charlevoix, Alpena and Wayne Counties, Michigan" prepared for the United States Department of the Interior by Commonwealth Cultural Resources Group, Inc. March, 2000.

Interview with Richard Clute of the Jesse Besser Museum.

CHAPTER III - LIGHTHOUSE

Northern Lights by Charles Hyde, 1986.

Chronology of Aids to Navigation – The Unites States Lighthouse Service 1716-1939 by Truman R. Strobridge from U.S. Coast Guard Historian's Office website - http://www.uscg.mil/hq/g-cp/history/collect.html.

Lighthouse Evolution and Typology by Dr. Robert Browning from U.S. Coast Guard Historian's Office website - http://www.uscg.mil/hq/g-cp/history/collect.html.

Alpena History Collection – Fred Trelfa – Alpena County Library.

Seeing the Light by Terry and Sue Pepper, website – http://www.terrypepper.com/lights/index.html.

History of Communications-Electronics in the United States Navy by Linwood S. Howeth, 1963.

Great Lakes Lighthouse Tales by Frederick Stonehouse, 1998.

Charting the Inland Seas by Arthur Woodford, 1991.

Sentries of the Sea by John J. Floher, 1942.

Excerpts from Annual Light Lists, Reports of the Lighthouse Board and Reports of the Lake Carriers Association – courtesy of Terry Pepper.

Lighthouses and Lightships by George R. Putnam, 1917.

Logbooks for Thunder Bay Island Lighthouse. Record Group 26,

National Archives, Old Military and Civilian Records, Washington, D.C.

"Diary of Henry West, 1828-1832" from Library, Winterthur Museum, Winterthur, Delaware.

CHAPTER IV – FISHING VILLAGE

Fishing the Great Lakes by Margaret Beattie Bogue, 2000.

Alpena History Collection – Fred Trelfa – Alpena County Library.

Thunder Bay National Marine Sanctuary website – http://www.glerl.noaa.gov/glsr/thunderbay.

Historical Tales of the Huron Shore, R.E. Prescott, 1934 - 1942.

"Seines to Salmon Charters – 150 years of Michigan Great Lakes Fisheries" by MSU Cooperative Extension Service, 1977.

"An Archeological Survey of Commercial Fisheries, Life Saving Station and Lighthouse Complex on the Thunder Bay Island Group" by Erin Williams, MSU Anthropology Department, 1997.

"Michigan's Commercial Fisheries of the Great Lakes" by John Van Oosten, Michigan History Magazine. Volume 22, 1938.

"The Journal of Paul Nelson Spoffard of New York City 1848," Michigan History Magazine. Volume 29, No. 3.

History of the Lake Huron Shore, 1883.

History of Alpena County, by William Boulton, 1876, from Collections of the Pioneer Society of the State of Michigan, Vol. VI.

Journals of John W. Paxton:
Shipwreck of the Schooner Sparrow – 1848
Journal – Schooner Marshal Ney – 1853
Journal – Schooner Alpha – 1856
Thunder Bay Island Law Docket – 1858
Journal – Sugar Island – 1859-1874
From Trelfa Collection at the Clarke Historical Library, Central Michigan University.

Captain John Paxton and His Journal (unpublished) by Rilla Whitten King, 1995.

Interview with Rilla Whitten King, February, 2004.

CHAPTER V – LIFESAVERS

A Legacy: The United States Life-Saving Service by Dr. Dennis L. Noble from U.S. Coast Guard Historian's Office website - http://www.uscg.mil/hq/g-cp/history/collect.html.

Wreck Ashore by Frederick Stonehouse, 1994.

Sand Pounders by Robert F. Bennett, U.S. Coast Guard, 1998

"The 26-foot-8-inch Self-Bailing Self-Righting Sailing, Pulling Lifeboat of the US Life-Saving Service" by William D. Wilkinson. Wreck and Rescue. Fall, 1977.

"Fred Poirier Captain Coast Guard Retires" Alpena News, October 21, 1929.
"Capt. Plough, Old Alpena Life Saver Due For Retirement" Alpena News, January 27, 1915.

Alpena History Collection – Fred Trelfa – Alpena County Library.

Wreck Reports of Thunder Bay Island Life Saving Station, microfilm published by the United States Archives available from the Alpena County Library.

Great Lakes – A Brief History of U.S. Coast Guard Operations by Dennis L. Noble, published by the Coast Guard Public Affairs Staff, 1989.
"Captain John B. Persons Recalls 38 years Battling Storms on Thunder Bay Island," by Stella Champney. The Detroit News, December 2, 1931.

CHAPTER VI – SHIPWRECKS

Charting the Inland Seas by Arthur Woodford, 1991.

Wreck Reports of Thunder Bay Island Life Saving Station, microfilm published by the United States Archives available from the Alpena County Library.

Annual Reports of the U.S. Life Saving Service – available from the Michigan Maritime Museum, South Haven, Michigan.

"The Sinking of the O.E. Parks" by E.G. Richardson in The Telescope, May/June 1975.

RG 26 Records of the U.S. Coast Guard – Logbooks of Stations 1876 – 1941, Thunder Bay Island, National Archives – Great Lakes Region (Chicago).

Labadie Collection - Thunder Bay Sanctuary Research Collection – Alpena County Library.

CHAPTER VII – COAST GUARD

"Coast Guard Children on Thunder Bay Island" by Kay Richardson, Wreck and Rescue, Fall, 1997.

Microfilm of Coast Guard Assistance Reports at Alpena County Library.

Interviews with James Messer and Ralph Gates – December, 2002.

United States Coast Guard Registers – various years available from Michigan Maritime Museum, South Haven, Michigan.

RG 26 Records of the U. S. Coast Guard – Logbooks of Stations 1876 – 1941, Thunder Bay Island, National Archives – Great Lakes Region (Chicago).

Correspondence with Bill Adrian, October, 2003.

Interview with Jack LaForest, December, 2003.

Interview with Walt Plohocky, January, 2004.

Interviews with Paul Rehkopf and Phyllis Richardson Everly, February, 2004.

CHAPTER VIII – PRESERVATION

Archives of Thunder Bay Island Preservation Society.